General editor: Graham Handley MA PhD

Brodie's Notes on

Chosen Poems of Thomas Hardy

Graham Handley MA PhD
Formerly Principal Lecturer and Head of English Department, The College of All Saints, Tottenham

This revised edition published 1986 by Pan Books Ltd
Cavaye Place, London SW10 9PG
9 8 7 6 5 4 3 2 1
© Graham Handley 1986
ISBN 0 330 50232 8
Photoset by Parker Typesetting Service, Leicester
Printed and bound in Great Britain by
Richard Clay (The Chaucer Press) Ltd, Bungay, Suffolk

Contents

Page references in these Notes are to
the Macmillan Students' edition of
Chosen Poems of Thomas Hardy, selected
and edited by James Gibson but as the poems
are analysed separately, the Notes may be used
with any edition of Hardy's poetry.

Preface

The intention throughout this study aid is to stimulate and guide, to encourage the reader's involvement in the text, to develop disciplined critical responses and a sure understanding of the main details in the chosen text.

Brodie's Notes on poetry texts begin by introducing the student to the author's life and works or, in the case of an anthology of poems, to each poet, his time, his main themes and other relevant material.

The Note will also provide a summary of each poem, together with a critical commentary on it in which there is particular reference to form, rhyme, rhythm or any poetic devices which seem to the editor to merit remarks, or which need evaluation. Textual notes will be explanatory or critical, sometimes both, defining what is difficult or obscure on the one hand, or stressing particular usages, figures of speech, themes or the main concerns of the poet. Revision questions will be set on each sequence of poems to test the student's careful application to the text of the prescribed book.

The paramount aim is to send the student back to the text. Each study aid will include a series of general questions which require a detailed knowledge of the set book; the first of these questions will have notes by the editor of what might be included in a written answer. A short list of books considered useful as background reading for the student will be provided at the end.

Graham Handley

The author and his work

Thomas Hardy was born on 2 June 1840 in a brick and thatch house at Upper Bockhampton, a hamlet in the parish of Stinsford near Dorchester in Dorset. Here his father, too, was born and died, and Hardy himself chose to spend most of his life near his roots, building himself a house – Max Gate – close by after his major literary successes. Hardy's father was a buoyant and kindly man, a master mason or builder, quite well off for most of his life, but lacking in ambition. He was devoted to his music – Hardys had played and sung the music at Stinsford Parish Church for over a hundred years – and this interest was communicated to and inherited by his son. Hardy's deep love of this traditional music is reflected in his portrait of the Mellstock choir in his early novel, *Under the Greenwood Tree* (1872). As a boy he learned to tune the fiddle, and played it as a young man at weddings and festivals. He would also join in the dancing, sometimes weeping with emotion.

He was greatly influenced by and devoted to his mother. She was an omnivorous reader and a strong character – 'the stuff of which great men's mothers are made', as a character in Hardy's powerful novel, *Far From the Madding Crowd* (1874) observes in his fictional world. Hardy was a delicate child, not expected to survive long after his birth, and he did not attend school until he was eight years old. But such was his mental precocity, together with the atmosphere of books and music in his home and the nature of the countryside around him, that he soon made progress. He had read Dryden's translation of Virgil and Dr Johnson's unusual novel *Rasselas* before he entered Dorchester day-school, where he won his first prize at the age of fourteen. He had already made great strides in Latin, and was soon able to read Virgil in the original. He went through Shakespeare, Scott, Milton and some of the popular novelists of his own day. Soon he was learning French and German, but it would be true to say that the Bible was perhaps his main area of study. He knew much of it by heart, and taught in the local Sunday school. He appears to have been popular at school, though in some ways he was of a withdrawn temperament, often giving himself to solitude. He gained much insight into the world around him; one of the macabre memories which was to remain with him was his seeing through a telescope the body of a woman who had been hanged. The traditions and rituals and superstitions of the villagers and their way of life were ever-present to the developing imagination of the boy. From them he was to create some of his great fiction and, in his eyes, his no less important poetry.

When he was twenty years old Hardy went into the offices of an ecclesiastical architect in Dorchester. Here he worked for a man named John Hicks, an employer who was himself cultured. Hardy formed the habit of getting up early to study, and added Greek to the Latin he had already acquired. One of his interesting and stimulating neighbours was William Barnes, a dialect poet, scholar and craftsman. A year later Hardy went to London, still working as an architect and restorer, but acquiring a much greater artistic culture from his stay in the capital. He visited art galleries and libraries and read widely in science and philosophy. He was influenced by Charles Darwin, whose *Origin of the Species* was published in 1859. By the age of thirty Hardy was intellectually an agnostic and, despite his architecturally based career – and he was certainly competent – he was turning to writing. He produced some verses and a novel, *The Poor Man and the Lady*, which was rejected by Macmillan. In 1871 he paid a firm to publish his next attempt in fiction, *Desperate Remedies*. It is an uneven and largely melodramatic piece of work, but it has a certain emotional power and the morbid tendency which was to characterize his much later fictional work in particular.

In 1872 he published *Under the Greenwood Tree*. Although this is a Wessex idyll, it has the rustic humour which is typical of Hardy, a loving and warm portrait of the Mellstock choir and of nature, as well as a wayward if sympathetic heroine in Fancy Day. *A Pair of Blue Eyes* (1873) shows a major advance in structure, having moments of poignant and lyrical intensity. During this time Hardy had met Emma Gifford on one of his church restoration tours; she was a religious and rather solitary woman, conscious that she was better born than Hardy. But despite this they were married in September 1874 on the strength of Hardy's next novel, *Far From the Madding Crowd*. This appeared in one of the leading magazines of the day, the *Cornhill*, being serialized from January to November 1874 before appearing in volume form. It was his first real success.

This was followed by *The Hand of Ethelberta* (1876), something of a failure, before the great novel, *The Return of the Native* (1878) established him as one of the finest novelists of the century and indeed of all time. As he wrote on, his mood grew progressively sombre and tragic. There were two great novels in the 1880s, *The Mayor of Casterbridge* (1886) and *The Woodlanders* (1887), both epitomizing the fated man. The first of these has the superb selling-of-the-wife-scene at the beginning which carries with it the terrible nemesis which overtakes the leading character, Michael Henchard. The second is notable for the loyalty and devotion of Marty South to the ill-fated and self-effacing Giles Winterborne. But it is impossible to do justice in two sentences to the complexity, craftsmanship and sheer imaginative verve of these novels. Set in his beloved Wessex, they are imbued with tragic irony, the ironies of personal interaction, of irrevocable decision, of human relationships caught in these decisions, and subject to circumstances and coincidences in which the presence of a malign fate is seen.

In 1891 the three-volume edition of *Tess of the D'Urbervilles* was issued, and it soon became Hardy's most popular novel, being translated into many languages and bringing, as so often with Hardy, controversy with it. One of its original pre-titles was *Too Late Beloved*, and two of the scenes involving Tess's midnight baptism of her child Sorrow, and the location of her seduction (or rape) by Alec D'Urberville, were cut from the serial version. This was to conform with Victorian prudery, but both were restored by Hardy in the book edition.

His final novel, *Jude the Obscure* (1895), christened by one critic *Jude the Obscene*, traces the struggles of a working man to get into Christminster (the thinly disguised name for Oxford) and his failure in life and in marriage. Again the intensity of the conception is tragic; Jude dies in poverty and obscurity, a martyr to man's inhumanity to man, particularly if that man is of a different class and background to those accepted as educable by society. The reception of this radical novel, with its direct challenge to a code of judgement which is fundamentally immoral, was largely bitter and hostile. As with *Tess*, it probed conventional conceptions of marital and sexual relationships with an unerring emphasis on truth at the expense of social and religious fallacies. Though he had for some years been settled at his home in Max Gate, and though he was now widely recognized as a great writer, Hardy turned his back on the novel, and devoted his literary energies to poetry, his first and deepest love.

At this period of his life there is little doubt that there was growing domestic disharmony between himself and his wife Emma. The marriage had been childless, she was aware of their (supposed) social differences, and even had delusions of her own grandeur which included the belief that she was a superior writer to her husband. Emma died in 1912, and Hardy was stricken with remorse, his poignant verse and his visits to places he had visited with her all those years ago testifying to his personal anguish. Nevertheless, in 1914 he married a woman nearly forty years his junior, Florence Dugdale, and took her home to Max Gate. Throughout their life he continued to write poems – often about Emma – sensitive, lyrical creations of exquisite concentration, craftsmanship and feeling. The greatest living novelist was hailed as a major poet, and there are still critics today who value Hardy's poetry above his prose.

Be that as it may, honours were showered upon him in his lifetime, especially after the publication of *The Dynasts*, a verse-drama of the Napoleonic Wars. He received a number of honorary degrees (ironic for a man who had never formally progressed beyond grammar school). The Order of Merit was bestowed on him in 1910, the Gold Medal of the Royal Society of Literature in 1911. His greatest pleasure perhaps came from his being granted the Freedom of the Borough of Dorchester. He himself supervised the reprinting of many of his works in his own lifetime, and left a considerable amount of money when he died. He had virtually written an autobiographical account of himself, though it was published as if his second wife had written it. The irony which pervades so much of his work was given a dramatic twist immediately after his death. It was decided that the man who had never sought fame should be buried in Westminster Abbey. There were quarrels over the precedence for tickets; the agnostic was buried in England's national shrine. The body was cremated, the ashes interred in Poet's Corner beneath a spadeful of Dorset earth, while his heart was carried back to Stinsford and buried in the grave of his first wife. This final act is consonant with his greatest fiction and his unique spirit.

Introduction

Dr James Gibson's edition of the *Chosen Poems of Thomas Hardy*, produced for schools, has for some years been a standard examination text and will continue to be so. In effect it is a carefully selected contraction of his *The Complete Poems of Thomas Hardy*. This is the definitive text of the poetry for the general reader, while for the specialist there is the Variorum Edition, which provides the variants in manuscript and in other editions.

Dr Gibson's *Chosen Poems* contains a fine introduction to Hardy's poetry, the notes on each poem being critical, factual and scholarly. The student should read Dr Gibson's notes before reading this particular commentary on the poems. You must regard the Brodie's Note as a supplement to Dr Gibson's work. Where he is silent, the student will perhaps find that I have added to the critical evaluation of each given poem by mentioning its form or structure, or a particular poetic technique, or that I have underlined a point made by Dr Gibson, or indicated a common Hardy theme. Your basic text is the *Chosen Poems*; your additional source of reference the Brodie's Note on that text.

Hardy is a great poet. He writes movingly about the past and indeed the present, he is both wise and nostalgic, and he has the special quality which marks the genuine poet – the ability to write with particularity but to universalize what he says as well. What is remarkable about him is his variety, his range of poetic forms and subjects. It is true that he uses traditional metres, but even when he does so his verse conveys his strong individuality of tone and emphasis. The first extract printed here *The Field of Waterloo* (p.27) exemplifies a number of Hardy qualities. There is his love of nature, something that runs throughout his verse; there is that sense of perspective which sees the creatures of nature set against the vast powers of man; there is a sense of history and particularity; there is the superb control of the chosen form; there is a tendency towards morbid contemplation of fate; there is the archaic usage of a word like 'Yea'. If we turn on exactly 100 pages in the *Chosen Poems* we find that the poem is

Weathers. This is much different in form to the extract we have just looked at from *The Dynasts*. After the first four lines with their alternate rhymes – one shorter line providing effective rhythmic and musical contrast with the longer line in pairs – there is a sequence of four lines having the same rhyming word. The repetition of the short second line, 'And so do I', makes the poem a lyric with a refrain. This is repeated in the second verse, where exactly the same rhyme scheme is employed, but the seasonal/weather contrast is enhanced by the regularity of the form, for despite changes it, like the seasons, has a permanence.

These two examples, briefly touched on here, indicate the qualities and the quality of Hardy's verse. You must bring to your reading of Hardy both your eyes and your ears, for Hardy is both a visual and an aural poet. Babette Deutsch, in her *Poetry Handbook*, refers to poetry as 'the art which uses words both as speech and song to reveal the realities that the senses record, the feelings salute, the mind perceives, and the shaping imagination orders.' This is finely definitive of Hardy's achievement, but poetry is also an individual voice which speaks to individual readers, and no two readers will respond in exactly the same way to a given set of experiences. The reader of Hardy's verse is set fair to taste a variety of moods, descriptions, responses, stories, autobiographical and psychological explorations, love of animals, speculations upon life. Make them your own experiences, and not the conveniently adopted views of a critic or teacher. The Notes on each poem are a guide to appreciation. If a poem is read with sensitivity and imagination, with insight and discipline – in short, with the head and the heart – much more than is recorded in the Notes will be discovered. The experience will be first hand, and all positive experience in life and in literature should be just that. The reader may disagree with a particular emphasis or even interpretation in the Notes: this, unless it results from obstinacy or lack of self-discipline, is a healthy sign, for it marks the beginning of critical awareness in the individual. And once this awareness has established itself in the mind, confident and balanced evaluations will be made, and the art of appreciation will become the major part of the reader's response to what he or she reads.

To return to Hardy, we must never forget that he was a writer steeped in local and literary traditions. In terms of poetical innovation, he is not a modern poet, though the views in his poems, like those expressed in his novels, are both modern and timeless. There is a kind of wisdom and irony in him that speaks of all times, and just as Hardy saw divinity in a blinded bird, so we see divinity in his poetry, whether it is personal, descriptive, or more than either of these. In terms of human enlightenment, the man who could subtitle his great novel *Tess of the D'Urbervilles* – in which the tragic heroine is hanged for the murder of her 'lover' – 'A Pure Woman Faithfully Presented', has much to say to our own age. And the man who could conceive *The Dynasts* on the one hand and write 'In Time of "The Breaking of Nations" ' on the other, embraces, like Shakespeare, the permanent truths of life as we know it. Hardy's poems complement his great novels in this signal achievement.

Literary terms used in these notes

A brief list of literary terms is given below. Make sure that you do not apply them loosely to the poem you are reading, since there is a danger that to speak of 'metaphors and similes', for example, will give the reader the false impression that he or she is 'appreciating' the poem being studied. Technical terms are useful only if their *function* is appreciated, if the way they heighten our response to a poem is defined.

Alliteration A phrase or succession of words beginning with the same letter, as in 'The Voice', where the poet speaks of '*f*altering *f*orward' and of 'wind oozing *th*in *th*rough *th*e *th*orn'.

Onomatopoeia This is where the words used reflect the sound of what is being described, as in '*oo*zing' above, and in another line from the same poem, 'Or is it only the breeze in its listlessness' where the *s*, *t* and *z* sounds combine to produce the effect of the noise of the breeze.

Ballad This is a song form with narrative, story content. It is often of a tragic nature (as in *A Sunday Morning Tragedy*, p.115). It is usually written in *quatrains,* verses having four lines each.

Metaphor A comparison which is implied but without using 'like' or 'as', the words which introduce the formal comparison of the *simile*. Take the poem 'The Darkling Thrush'. This is rich in metaphors – Frost is 'spectre-grey' (comparison with a ghost), Winter has 'dregs', the day coming to an end has a 'weakening eye'. A simile is seen in the comparison of the bine-stems, which are 'Like strings of broken lyres'.

Personification This is when the poet endows inanimate or abstract things with human qualities or effects. In 'The Darkling Thrush' Frost, Winter and the Century are each personified. When personification is used, there is normally a capital letter, though if you look at a poem like 'The Convergence of the Twain' (p.63) you will find that the sunken Titanic is personified throughout as in 'stilly couches she', 'her salamandrine fires', while the 'Shape of Ice' which sinks her is called 'a sinister mate' and the two are brought together in an 'intimate welding', being 'twin halves of one august event'.

Notes on individual poems will indicate particular forms or techniques where these are felt to be helpful in evaluating the qualities of the poem.

Critical commentaries, textual notes and revision questions on the poems

The sequence followed in this commentary is that of the text from pages 27–149. The title of the poem is given, followed by some general remarks where appropriate and then a glossary of individual words or phrases, images or techniques.

Note The student is advised to read James Gibson's notes *fully* before following what is written here.

Poems mainly autobiographical

The Field of Waterloo
(from *The Dynasts*)

The Dynasts is written from a range of viewpoints, from the mighty, like Napoleon, to the low, like the Wessex labourer. Here the three-line verses sometimes run into one another, and thus reflect the terrible movement of battle just as the rhythm of the lines reflects the 'thud of hoofs' and the movement of wheels. The poem is imbued with compassion, and the suffering in nature is balanced by the parallel that runs throughout: the senseless suffering of man. The last verse is particularly emphatic here, for the wheat and the flowers that will never reach full growth are a direct comparison with the dead who will not grow on into the fullness of life.

The alternate lines rhyming and the movement described above, together with the vivid and visual colour effects, somehow convey the excitement of battle and the terrible pathos attendant on the dumb creatures whose fragility will be broken by it.

hamlet-roofs i.e. of the villages.
tunnelled chambers . . . household . . . worms asks i.e. the animal world is endowed with human associations, and this gives poignancy and a certain pathos to the conception.
guesses him Believes that he is.
foul red rain Blood.
weather-foe As you read on, you will notice that one of Hardy's techniques is the coinage of double-barrelled words which, economically, or poetically or both, extend associations by being joined. His great sympathy for nature, for animals, is very evident here.
greened . . . gold . . . bud . . . bloom Apart from the parallel with man, note the running alliteration which is one of the major facets of Hardy's manner. A close look at the rest of this poem will show how consummately it is used for emphasis – and often how unobtrusively.

One We Knew
(M.H. 1772–1857)

Ballad-form poem of eight four-line verses which initially captures the speed of the dance in the length of its lines, the excitement of youth, and then varies the line according to the content – reminiscent, nostalgic, evocative of the mood of the past from the point of view of the child on whom his grandmother made such an abiding impression. The poem is a compound of vivid word-pictures and of the *sounds* of the past as well, and the key-line is 'Past things retold were to her as things existent'. Folk-song and ballad, in terms of rhythm and refrain as well as narrative, were of great importance to Hardy.

cots Cottages.

sod Turf.

figures The pattern of the dance.

To choose each other for good There is an inherent simplicity in this, almost a nostalgic wish that youth and the love of youth could be permanent. Note that it was written in 1902, when Hardy's first marriage would have been at low ebb.

the King of France Louis XVI, guillotined on 21 January 1793.

the Terror The orgy of bloodshed in the French Revolution which lasted from May 1793 to July 1794.

Bonaparte's unbounded His rise was spectacular, from that of Captain of artillery at Toulon in 1793, first consul by 1799, and consul for life in 1802.

his threats i.e. of invading England.

southern strand South coast.

a small child's shrieking Whether at the lightning, or being beaten, or watching the horse beaten, we are not to know – it is just a vivid evocation of a *felt*, remembered incident.

cap-framed Simple, effective coinage. The headdress would be worn indoors by women at this time.

But rather as one who sees i.e. because they are present to her, as he makes clear in the final verse.

no tongue could hail She is living in her own world of the past, but there is an implication that many she knew are dead, beyond the reach of the 'tongue'.

Past things retold . . . Things present . . . Note the fine antithetical balance, the consummate economy of expression, with the balance between the past and the present effectively enclosing the poem through the climax at the end. All life is, in fact, compounded of the past and the present.

Domicilium

This early exercise already shows Hardy's interest in the past and in nature. A simply expressed poem in blank verse, with a marked influence of Wordsworth in the manner of writing about nature, and a direct echo of some lines in *Tintern Abbey*. Even thus early Hardy had a sense of structure, for the initial descriptions are in short blank-verse paragraphs, which move from the house, the garden, the field and beyond to the 'wilder' scene. The fourth paragraph is longer, since it dwells on the past beyond the past (i.e. his grandmother's as distinct from his own), while the poem closes on the note of the wildness of that distant past. 'A human life', wrote George Eliot, 'should be well rooted in some spot of a native land', and here we have Hardy's roots, simply and lovingly expressed. Note the easy mastery of the relaxed and conversational tone, the genuine love of nature and the imaginative treatment of it, as in such a phrase as 'a veil of boughs'. There is an unforced naturalness about the grandmother's story too.

sprout a wish Simple personification, but underlining the strong emphatic feeling Hardy has for nature.
box Evergreen shrub.
esculents Something that is eatable; the word is unusual, and here employed with a kind of 'literary' self-consciousness.
Dropped by some bird This sense of time, of continuity, is one of the marks of the 'universality' of Hardy's verse.

A Church Romance
(Mellstock: about 1835)

The sonnet form deftly employed here, with the lightness of touch in the octave balanced by the heavier, longer lines symbolic of age and the changes it has wrought in the sestet. The language is simple, but insistently alliterative, reflecting the music which is so much a part of the romance. Note the visual quality of the scene, so strong that it can be recalled to memory with exactitude.

despite Notwithstanding the opposition of (her pride).
hearts' bond . . . signed i.e. they were (later) married. But 'bond' carries the half-weight of 'bondage', and is thus ironically used.

Age had scared Romance Heavy personification to underline the
  burden of the change.
Bowing i.e. playing the viol, but unusually employed as a verbal form
  here. Note that the sonnet ends with a couplet, an emphatic rounding-
  off of their lives.

The Roman Road

A short poem of fifteen lines, for the most part in rhyming
couplets, but with a refrain line – as in a song, 'The Roman
Road' – thus emphasizing the permanence of what is man-made,
though the changes which time brings are stressed. The second
line echoes another scene description – of man against the
background of nature – in Chapter 2 of Hardy's novel *The
Return of the Native*, where 'the long, laborious road, dry, empty,
and white . . . bisected that vast dark surface like the parting-line
on a head of black hair'. In Hardy, we always return to the
human. There are some superb alliterative effects ('Visioning on
the vacant air') but notice that the real nostalgia is that of personal tradition, the association with the poet's mother balancing,
so to speak, the wider perspective of history.

delve Dig.
Visioning i.e. seeing. Another verbal usage.
brass helmed Double-barrelled coinage, with 'helm' being archaic for
  'helmet'. Hardy frequently uses archaisms to underline the continuity,
  the permanence of tradition, which plays so great a part in his
  philosophy of life.

Childhood among the Ferns

Again the use of the triplets (three-line rhyming verses, though
differing from those in ·'The Field of Waterloo'), full of
descriptive touches which have the immediacy of recall: the
scene, the day, the sentiments are recaptured with vividness and
yet with an apparently effortless ease of expression and association. It is a moment of childhood with which many of us would
feel in sympathy, and because of that its basic appeal lies in the
fact that it says for us what we then felt. Yet despite the sureness
of the touch for the most part, there is something bathetic about
the end of the poem, perhaps because the word 'perambulate' is
itself unpoetic.

sprinkling Notice the effect of the word – immediately arresting in terms of sensation.

tall-stemmed ferns . . . tall ferns Hardy is deceptively simple in his use of repetition, here to convey the child's perspective.

lopping Hanging limply.

conned Strictly it means 'studied', and in the sense of storing in the memory, the word fits admirably here.

spray-roofed Fine double-barrelled epithet to convey the effect of the rain.

anon Archaic for 'soon, presently'.

I could live on here thus till death The strongly felt wish to remain within his 'roots' and the experience of nature. Again the influence of Wordsworth is apparent.

queried . . . sate Ask myself . . . sat. Hardy has used the archaic word here.

And this afar-noised World perambulate Inverted word order, indicating that he does not wish to grow up. The double-barrelled coinage contrasts with the peace of the scene, while 'perambulate' shows Hardy's capacity to employ the unusual word for effect.

The Oxen

Simple ballad-form poem concealing in its deceptive simplicity of language a deep and abiding concern for life and faith, linking the animal kingdom in its natural humility, with man in his faith, on the most significant night of the year – and at the same time expressing the poet's own doubts and yet his wish to be associated with worship. It is a poignant and nostalgic poem, deservedly much anthologized. Its universality conveys doubt and hope; a wry appraisal of man's inherent uncertainty; a moving sense of the loss of the innocent acceptance that is ours in childhood. Again there is a sure sense of realism conveyed through the conversational tone and the wistful nostalgia.

Now they are all on their knees This poem has a fine duality – the reference is to the oxen, the association with those praying in church.

elder Note the biblical word, giving a kind of patriarchal touch.

sat in a flock Note the transference of the word from beasts to people, a further underlining of the duality.

by the embers Favourite Hardy usage, redolent of the warmth of family life.

hearthside ease Immediate contrast of man with the oxen.

meek mild Note that the words, normally applied to the Virgin Mary, are deliberately used of the oxen.

there . . . then Always the context of time and place stressed.
doubt The word subtly prepares us for the poet's own uncertainty
  about his faith.
So fair a fancy i.e. such an imaginative idea.
Hoping The wish expressed is also that of the desire to return to
  childhood which nurtured faith in all its simplicity.

The Colour

Note the simplicity of the language, the use of repetition and
alliteration, the lilting musical effect in the rhythm and the
establishing of a sequence which reflects the changes and movements of life. Verse 1, for example, links white with weddings,
verse 2, red with soldiers (i.e. their red coats), verse 3, blue with
sailors, verse 4, green with celebrations on May Day, ending with
black for death in the last verse. Frequently ballads are in
dialogue, and this is a good example of the question-answer
balance preserved in so many of them. In a sense the poem
follows the life sequence, though less elaborate, more earthy and
of the people, of Shakespeare's 'All the world's a stage'.

Afternoon Service at Mellstock
(About 1850)

Again the four-line verse or quatrain is employed. These are
regular, but there is an interesting emphasis in the third line of
each verse, where the length of the line matches the singing and
the thinking which is a looking away from it. Again, the content
is imbued with a wistfulness for the days of childhood, and a
pondering on the limitations of the life of thought. It contains
some fine things – 'one-voiced' to reflect the unison of the choir,
the repetition which echoes the psalm, and some individual
coinages characteristic of Hardy's individual manner: 'out-
pourings', 'psalmings'. Alliteration, a kind of musical accom-
paniment, runs throughout.

Cambridge New The name of the tune.
whiles Occasions.
swaying like the trees The simile effectively expresses the harmony
  between man and nature.
mindless Hardy is very fond of 'ess' endings, and coins some of his

own, but here what he is conveying is that we do so many things – like singing – without realizing what we are doing or the significance of what is being sung.

psalming Again the use of a noun in verbal form, for emphasis.

A Wet Night

The writer records his experiences of a wet night, feeling his own hardship in the walk through the rain, but pondering on how his forebears took such a thing for granted as part of the routine of their lives. This sonnet, instead of ending with an emphatic closing couplet, has its sestet with alternate rhymes which somehow reflect the ongoing nature of past experience.

rain-shafts riddling Hardy often describes rain, but here the usage implies force – for instance 'arrows' initially – and the alliteration is as continuous as the rain itself. 'Riddling' means 'as through a coarse sieve'.

clams me, mire-bestarred Good combination of the real and the poetic – 'clams' meaning 'clogged with dampness', while the second epithet indicates the mud and the glistening drops of rain on it.

shades Darkness, gloominess.

calendared Again a Hardy coinage, meaning 'to be recorded' and remembered.

sires i.e. forebears.

beset, ere . . . shapen Note the use of archaisms, words that are appropriate here, since Hardy is dealing with the past; and here meaning 'happened', 'before' and 'made' respectively.

toils as trifles mere i.e. labourings, strivings as everyday occurrences. Note that by inverting the word-order ('trifles mere') Hardy has avoided the cliché.

The Self-Unseeing

Ballad in much shorter lines in which particular moments of the past are recalled. The alliterative effects are finely judged; the soft 'f's of the first verse giving way to the 'd' and 'b' of the last, which fit the joy of the experience and the dance. The language is simple, again until the last verse, where there is a temporarily heightened usage, 'emblazoned' to qualify the then-unrealized ecstasy.

Hardy has succeeded in conveying both the musical delight of the past and the evanescent quality of that past, though perhaps with the compensation that it can be recalled, as here.

dead feet Hardy has transferred the epithet with economical force – feet that are *now* dead.
emblazoned This is the heightened word – strictly speaking it means 'to adorn with heraldic devices', but more commonly to 'celebrate' or 'extol'.
Yet we were looking away! The exclamation shows how important the phrase is – Hardy is registering the fact that they did not realize how wonderful the moment was. Perhaps his own eyes were on the future.

Old Furniture

The play of the imagination, the influences and associations of memory, ultimately end in a self-denigratory conclusion, but throughout the poem there is the mastery of an unusual verse form (five-line), which ends in each case with a short and emphatic statement. The now familiar nostalgia is apparent, but the last verse gives the poem a somewhat different slant to those we have read hitherto. The penultimate verse, in fact, prepares us for the mood of the last verse, and the emphasis on the passage of time is typical of Hardy's perspective.

fashioning Style, make.
As in a mirror a candle-flame This is a fine verse which gives the perspective of the mind's eye in memory – clear in focus though the outlines may be progressively dimmer.
A foggy finger This poem is strongly alliterative, but this is one of the fainter images in the mirror of memory, hence the use of the adjective 'foggy'.
fingers are dancing Subtle association, for the viol set people dancing.
My father's Note the implication of the personal and universal here.
cut . . . gut Note the brief hard sounds of the rhymes, which echo the crispness of the playing.
in fits Abbreviation for 'in fits and starts' i.e. every 'now and again'.
stark Quite, wholly – very effective, sudden usage here.
Well, well . . . But sink away Paraphrased, this means that there is no time in the present to dwell on the past; those who do nothing but reminisce or live in the past should either get on with life or pass quietly away. Hardy's tacit implication is ironical, almost self-pitying, in view of his own chosen association with the past that made him: the places, the people, the things.

To Lizbie Browne

This is an exquisite song, shot through with the suggestion of what might have been that characterizes so much of Hardy's verse. Again the lightness is deceptive, for it covers an experience hitherto unvoiced; and the major part of what was *not* said is recaptured again in the next poem. There is a fine balance here between what is remembered, what is hypothetical, what happened and what might have happened. The result is a lyric of surpassing wistfulness, a melodic memory given permanence by being cast in words. The lines are short, for the time of youth and opportunity is short; the repetition and the refrain show how often the image of the subject has been repeated in the poet's mind. The subtle variations within the constriction of the verse form show Hardy's ingenuity, his feeling for the play of words and the associations set up by them. Strangely, with all the nostalgia, it is a poem of youth: the subject a child of nature; the song sprinkled with an alliterative flair that makes it easy on the tongue and the ear.

archly wile i.e. coyly cunning.
glance-giving Once more the economic coinage which says so much so directly.
Bred out of doors The simple recall is to the enhancing simplicity of nature.
By stealth to one i.e. secretly (to him).
swift . . . slow A play on 'The race is to the swift', here with ironic self-regret.
Girls ripen fast True, and the image again links her with the natural background of her 'ripening'.

Faintheart in a Railway Train

Very similar to the previous poem in theme – ironic appraisal of what might have been – but here based on an even more precarious incident. Two five-line verses, with a repetitive opening to each line of the first verse; and a stressed sequence which goes from town, to nature, to the girl seen. This leads naturally to the second verse, where he lacks the courage and enterprise to get out of the train and approach the 'radiant stranger'; and the final exclamation is one of regret. Note the exact passage of time in the factual journey, which approximates to a journey through life, the girl representing the way, the direction that might have been taken. The poem is remarkable both for its outer and inner perspective.

smirch Stain.
in my search for a plea i.e. trying to find an excuse (for speaking to her).

At a Lunar Eclipse

This poem is a sonnet, the first part of the octave (lines 1–4) being descriptive of the eclipse itself; the second (lines 5–8) questioning the relationship between this manifestation and the earth as he, the poet, knows it. In the sestet – which is divided into two three-line questions – and throughout the final part, the contrast between the shape of the earth and its inward turmoil is stressed. The poem is thus tightly structured, following a logical, if distressing, sequence. A heavy and somewhat morbid alliteration runs throughout. Note that the questions are rhetorical, that is, they go unanswered. This is a form of irony which underlines the poet's somewhat cynical contemplation of the vastness of the universe beside the smallness of man and the experiences of man which seem so large to him.

monochrome i.e. in one colour.
sun-cast symmetry i.e. as round and as smooth as the sun, which is responsible for casting the earth's shadow on the moon.
form . . . profile . . . brow Notice that the earth is personified, its reality being given human shape by association. The movement from the personal to the all-embracing (see 'continents' in the next line) is one of the features of the poem.
yon arc i.e. the eclipse.
Nation at war with nation i.e. the affairs of mankind, warfare, thinking, being brave or beautiful, are of small moment when seen against the vastness of space.

Neutral Tones

Perhaps the finest evocation of a mood in Hardy's verse, achieved by a consummate re-creation of a scene and an atmosphere consonant with the mood of the lovers. The first verse sets the scene, which is unusual in that the colours are 'neutral' rather than positive; it prepares us for the exchanges, largely unverbalized, between the lovers. The second verse is characterized firstly by the silence of the looks between them, and then – a superb technical achievement – the strained nature of the words when they do speak. Here the word-order underlines the nature of the experience they are suffering. The third verse describes the dead smile and the 'grin of bitterness', while the final verse shows the poet, in the light of experience, looking back on the sharp outlines of a scene which will recur, with all that it symbolizes, in his memory. Note the end-stopped lines in each of the verses, conveying the finality of the statements *and* the situation of the lovers. Note also the use of hard consonants throughout to evoke the mood, and also the technique whereby the first and last lines rhyming in each verse form a kind of enclosure, the enclosed experience of the lovers.

chidden Scolded or rebuked, archaic here. Notice that the term is strengthened in line 15 to 'God-curst'.

tedious riddles The implication is of unanswered questions, the tiresome exploration of their situation.

On which lost the more by our love The exact meaning is not clear, but the strain and tedium of the exchanges is reflected in the uncertain word-order.

Like an ominous bird a-wing A simile which indicates the death of love, the bird being a bird of prey. The scene is thus symbolic of a tortured goodbye.

wrings with wrong Note the fine alliteration to stress the squeezing out, torturing nature of the experience.

In a Eweleaze near Weatherbury

Fine lyrical touch from Hardy as, at the age of fifty, he recaptures once more the essential nature of an early love-experience. The form is simple, with three eight-line verses, each having alternate lines rhyming. He dwells on the fact that, though he has changed in terms of age, in basic response to life he is unchanged. He would still worship Beauty, though he records wryly that it would not reply to him in the language of past love. The running alliteration and the relaxed and simple nature of the verse both contribute to the musicality of the effect. It is light, whimsical, nostalgic and wise.

Eweleaze A grass field or down stocked with sheep.
kindled gaily Love's fitful ecstasies i.e. happily moved me to love her.
feature . . . fantasies i.e. the aspect in my dreams.
never-napping A quietly effective coinage – Time never rests or 'naps'.
I'd go . . . Beauty I'd do anything. The personification of Beauty
  appears to refer to youthful love and everything associated with it, i.e.
  it is both particular and general.
balm the breeze i.e. sweeten it.
Thine for ever i.e. I will be yours (true to you) for ever. And when he
  dies he will be able to look back with enjoyment.

Great Things

A light-hearted romp expressing great joy in life, in drink,
cycling, dancing and love, the final verse summarizing these
'great' things to be had before death. It is a song dependent on
repetition and the refrain, its zest being its main quality. Note
the internal rhyme which maintains the joyful lilting quality, and
notice also the sheer happiness and ecstasy present – positive
reflections of an optimism which is not that common in Hardy.

hostelry i.e. public house.
flits like one a-wing i.e. comes towards me lightly like a bird. Compare
  the image with the one used in the previous poem.
One will call, 'Soul, I have need of thee' i.e. the onset of death.
Joy-jaunts i.e. drinking and cycling.

'When I set out for Lyonnesse'

The very name of Lyonnesse has legendary associations, for it
was supposedly the scene of many incidents in the Arthurian
story and in the romances of Tristan and Iseult. It is very
important in Cornish tradition and folklore, and all this is
present in the *language* of Hardy's fine lyric. Although it is about
a personal journey, the use of archaisms and the choice of words
like 'lonesomeness' and 'fathomless' remind one of the timeless
quality of the scene. In fact, the past informs the present, almost
as if a knight has gone in quest of his lady and won her love. The
verses are of six lines each, repetition and alliteration run
throughout; the first verse deals with the journey; the second
with the guesses at what happened while he was there; and the
third registers his return 'With magic in my eyes!'.

bechance Archaic – it really means 'happen' here.
wisest wizard A deliberate invocation of the past and of folklore
  (perhaps a glance at the legendary Merlin of Arthurian romance).
All marked Everyone noticed.
fathomless i.e. which could not be guessed at.

The Sun on the Bookcase
(Student's Love-song: 1870)

Two seven-line verses, the first purely descriptive of the room
and of nature outside. The second is rather different in tone,
arguing finally that time has not been wasted; for when the poet
has achieved what he has to he will be able to claim his loved one.
It has none of the elevation of the previous poem – the journey
is of the imagination – but it does record an experience common
to many who are separated. The handling of the rhyme-scheme,
as ever in Hardy, is superb, and the theme which links the
present with the nostalgic love has a certain poignant touch,
since one is left wondering whether the writer will achieve any of
his 'great deeds'.

the boiling ball i.e. the sun.
imaged i.e. formed the image of, pictured in one's mind's eye
anon Presently (archaic).
alway Always (archaic).

'We Sat at the Window'
(Bournemouth, 1875)

Two eight-line verses, with varying length of line and an
elaborate rhyme scheme: the first descriptive of the day, which
sets the mood; the second descriptive of the couple as they
reflect the mood. It is a kind of domesticated 'Neutral Tones',
but completely lacking the intensity and the emotional tautness
of that poem. Nevertheless it conveys the emotional, sympathetic dissonance between the couple very well, and might be
contrasted with the earlier poem; it is almost as if the habit of life
together has muted any natural outgoing. The choice of the
exact day is particularly appropriate and, typically, the rain is
consonant with the present mood of the couple and indicates the
'bad weather' of their relationship.

like silken strings Note the various descriptions Hardy gives of rain –
'silken' perhaps conveys domestic bondage or intensity.

witless things But the image is ironic – the couple themselves have
'wits' but don't use them to each other, and the couple are unhappy in
their silence and passivity.

We were irked by the scene Note the longer line as the poem becomes
reflective.

waste One of Hardy's favourite words to describe the inability to
realize fully a moment in time and to enjoy it.

A January Night
(1879)

A short poem with two themes: first, the description of the night
outside; then the supernatural association of the night with the
man recently dead. Three verses, alternate lines rhyming, with a
vivid personification of nature at the beginning (not unlike a sick
person in its outburst); and the implication that perhaps nature
reflects in its agony the agony of the dead man's spirit. Very
simple language, ending with the enigma of ignorance.

smites Note the heavy alliterative effects and also those of
personification, so that the wind and the rain become a creature.

Writhes This word sets in train the 'dread' associations which the poet
cannot account for.

The Last Signal
(11 October 1886) A Memory of William Barnes

The technical qualities are fully indicated in this note by J. G.
William Barnes (1800–86) wrote many poems whose subject
matter overlaps Hardy's own, and throughout his verse runs a
rich love of nature and a strongly compassionate tone. Hardy
edited the Select *Poems of William Barnes*, choosing what to include
in the edition himself. The lyrical tone, but with considerable
technical virtuosity, predominates; *The Milkmaid O' The Farm* is a
good example, a simple Tess situation without the tragedy.

And dark was the east The inverted word order perhaps symbolizes
the end of a life.

athwart Across.

grave-way A fine brief coinage to indicate 'on his way to be buried'.

Shelley's Skylark
(The Neighbourhood of Leghorn: March 1887)

Shelley's 'Ode to a Skylark' ('Hail to Thee, blithe spirit!') is imbued with the poet's individual lyrical meditations. Hardy, by way of contrast, speculates on the bird that inspired them: the one bird, of course, symbolizing the many. The poem is in quatrains, has some superb turns of phrase but, it must be confessed, some rather obvious literary 'conceits', or far-fetched references. Note the bathos of 'Go find it, faeries' and 'a bard to win'.

oblivious eyeless i.e. unseen and unknown, the term almost echoed at the end of the first verse.

through times to be i.e. all time.

when piped farewell i.e. sang its last notes.

throbs in a myrtle's green Imaginative phrase, the skylark 'feeding' the evergreen shrub, with white-scented flowers, sacred to Venus.

the coming hue/Of a grape Again the imaginative association, 'coming' finely conveying the development of ripeness.

Ecstatic heights We might note that the heights are the skylark's too, or, in the words of Shelley, 'That from Heaven or near it . . .'

At the Pyramid of Cestius near the Graves of Shelley and Keats
(1887)

Although this poem is in four-line verses, it is technically striking because of the very long third line in each verse which contains the substance of the poet's thought. The opening has an echo ('Who is Sylvia, what is she?' from Shakespeare's early comedy *The Two Gentlemen of Verona*), and the poet seems to be trying to achieve a balance between the conversational tone and a certain elevation required by the subject.

One thought alone brings he Inverted word order, perhaps reflecting history's inverted decision on Cestius.

Whose purpose was expressed The pyramid was designed to glorify the memory of Cestius, but instead it glorifies the memory of two poets unknown to him.

history-haunted Keats, too, employed the double-barrelled epithet, so Hardy has chosen, appropriately here, the coinage conveying the mixed history of Rome from pre-Christian times.

matchless singers i.e. Keats and Shelley.

– Say, then Note the admirable, clear-cut language of this verse, as compact as the pyramid, as clear as the fame of the two poets.

The Division

Moving love poem and, though the physical distance between the lovers is not as important as 'that thwart thing', it is ironic that it was also the distance to Lyonnesse. Each of the verses is an exclamation of anguish, the weather being almost incidental to the inward tumult. The poem is characterized by unusual words: 'severance', 'thwart' and the archaic 'betwixt'; but in terms of balance and passion it is a poignant lyric. There is, too, a terrible finality about it. Note the relaxed conversational tone which is itself an ironic comment on the intensity of the inward feelings.

A Broken Appointment

Again the poignant note is sounded, but here the emphasis on form tends to detract from the sincerity of utterance. The first and final lines of each of the two verses are the same, giving the effect, almost, of a foreshortened *rondeau* (see for example Leigh Hunt's 'Jenny Kissed Me'). Having said that, let us add that the theme is vital to any understanding of Hardy the man, the 'lovingkindness' so rightly stressed in James Gibson's note. There is therefore a high sense of loss, not in the conventional sense, but of loss to the human spirit which does not live in 'lovingkindness'. The fact that the poem ends with a question, already answered, adds to the pathos.

hope-hour Another fine economical coinage to underline anxiety.
love alone can lend you loyalty The core of Hardy's belief – and note the exquisitely soft alliteration in which it is expressed.
time-torn See 'hope-hour' (line 7) for the same effect of racked with anxiety.

The Impercipient
(At a Cathedral Service)

In effect, this is a hymn in defence of doubt, sensitively using some of the associations of faith to mark the writer's own consciousness, regret and natural humility. It is a beautifully balanced poem, but there is a moving sense of isolation about it too – as if the man who stands in a congregation is even more conscious of his difference as a non-believer than if he had never gone to church! Here, Hardy's known affiliation with what is traditional should also be taken into account. The structure – effectively alternate lines rhyming, short and long – is brought to an abrupt end in the final two lines; as abrupt, one might say, as death.

mirage-mists i.e. delusions.
consigned i.e. delivered.
Abides i.e. remains.
I am like a gazer There is some difficulty here. The verse seems to mean that, to some, the wind in the trees will symbolize the sea – because of its noise, associations. There is perhaps even the idea of a mast at sea, made from a like tree. Others, like Hardy, will merely see a tree and nothing beyond. Some see evidence of their faith everywhere; others, like the poet, merely see things for what they are.
upfingered Again the economical expressive coinage.
But for the charge i.e. the poet resents being taxed with the accusation that he would rather not believe in divine goodness, for it is not true – it would be tantamount to saying that a bird that has no wings deliberately seeks out the earth, whereas in fact it cannot fly above it anyway.
disquiet Doubt, uncertainty. Note the superb economy of the ending, the 'Rest shall we' which is synonymous with the eternal rest – death.

The Going of the Battery
Wives' Lament (2 November 1899)

Ballad with internal rhyme and the regular rhythm mentioned in the previous sentence, the style somewhat reminiscent of the Victorian minor poet Thomas Hood. The final effect is that of stoicism in the face of adversity: moved though Hardy was, the sentiments are idealized rather than realistic.

Hardy often uses the unusual word – here a word like 'unblenchingly' carries its own force, and the running alliteration contributes to the lilting effect. Unfortunately, the poem is somewhat undermined by affectedly poetic lines like 'Not to court perils that honour could miss', while the actual quoted words of one of the women sound unrealistic.

Light in their loving i.e. flitting, not stable or true.

the South Sea Presumably the Mediterranean, or any sea that has to be crossed.

living things seeming there The idea is extended in the next line, but the terrible irony is that they are takers of life.

tar-cloths . . . upmouthed Note again the effect of the 'humanizing' of what is made to destroy, part of an ironic overtone.

blank . . . prophetic An extension of the idea above. They are 'blank' at the moment.

Hand i.e. God.

Other and graver things i.e. the fear (in the small hours of the morning) that their men will not return.

Drummer Hodge

The contemplation of death in war, the fate of the ordinary man, is the theme here. There is a strikingly individual vocabulary and touch employed in this poem, though the structure – three six-line verses with alternate lines rhyming – has been used in previous poems. The simplicity emphasizes the sudden simplicity of death. Nature and the heavens provide the background and foreground to the poem; for they are permanent, whereas man's life is transitory.

They throw in Notice the lack of dignity, undoubtedly used as a contrast with the formal pomp common at funerals of those who die at home in peacetime.

kopje . . . veldt . . . Karoo All emphasize the foreignness to Hodge.

Hodge The name is traditionally typical of the English country labourer. Implicitly Hardy is comparing his natural occupation with where he ends; unnaturally, for this earth is foreign to him. And, as we see from the previous verse, 'foreign' constellations are above him.

unknown Hardy is fond of using the negative, this time with sardonic irony: Hodge, being dead, cannot 'know' where he is buried, and note that this word echoes the 'uncoffined' of the first verse.

strange-eyed constellations There is a clever transference of the double-barrelled 'strange-eyed' here, since they would only be strange to the dead soldier if he could see them. A further underlining of the pathos of the simple man dying far from all he knows.

The Man He Killed

Another aspect of the theme of war: the short four-line verses virtually in the shape of a monologue; the whole presenting the ironic but essentially true idea that a man does not hate his foe, he merely kills him. Behind this there is the additional social comment – the casual way that men enlist, or the poverty that forces them to do so.

to wet i.e. drink.
Just so There are three breaks in two lines here – a subtle indication that the soldier has difficulty in reasoning out the rights of the matter of war.
'list i.e. enlist, join up.
Off-hand like i.e. casually, without thinking.
traps Trappings, bits and pieces.
quaint . . . curious Both words are inadequate to describe the horror of war, and therefore carry their own irony.
where any bar is Once more the reversed word order is effective, for war itself reverses standards.

The Darkling Thrush

Four eight-line verses, though effectively each verse consists of two quatrains with alternate lines rhyming. The poem is rich in imagery, personification and contrasts. Its focus is on the landscape as compared with the one thing that is not consonant in mood with it – the song of the thrush. The latter is redolent of hope, while the landscape, frost-bound, is desolate. In the first verse the poet, alone, contemplates the scene; while in the second the compelling atmosphere overcomes him so he is 'fervourless', deprived of animation. Verse three marks the sudden transition, the joyful song of the bird belying its appearance. In verse four the poet ponders on the contrast between song and scene and the unknown and animating spirit of the thrush.

Frost was spectre-grey Notice the personification and the fact that it is nearly night, when spectres might appear – an imaginative connection in the poet's mind, since it anticipates the 'spectre' of the thrush.
dregs i.e. sediment, what is left; sap fallen to its lowest level.
scored Cut or scratched.
Like strings of broken lyres The simile is particularly apt, since there is no music in the scene until the thrush begins to sing.
haunted Reiteration of ghostliness and death.
The land's sharp features . . . his death-lament These four lines, a sequence of personificiation, make the landscape 'dead' by using traditional associations of burial – the crypt and the lament, for example – and there is a fine running alliteration of hard 'c's which are as crisp and stiff in sound as is the frost in reality.

The ancient pulse Notice that the personification is continued, to stress the absence of any life-force in the scene.

fervourless The effectiveness here is by contrast with the landscape, since fervour means 'heat' or 'passion'.

At once Note the clever use of rising rhythm to convey exultaton.

evensong This simple word, evocative of Christian worship, invests the thrush with a spiritual quality.

blast-beruffled Splendid coinage to indicate the survival powers of the thrush against the winter storms.

fling his soul This means simply to 'sing with all his heart', but 'fling' is a splendid choice of word since the thrush himself has been 'flung' by the 'blast'.

carolings Carols are sung in praise of the birth of Christ; there is a touch of irony in its usage here, for there appears to be nothing to praise in the landscape, though again the spiritual quality of the bird's song is evident.

terrestrial Earthly, contrasting with the spiritual.

blessed Hope 'Hope springs eternal in the human breast', wrote Pope, but Hardy chooses to stress the bird's intuitive sense of the coming of spring. The mood of the poet is sombre, as unhopeful as that of the landscape, whereas the bird's song is redolent of joy.

To an Unborn Pauper Child

Birth is a favourite subject for poets, and the interested student might like to compare Hardy's fine poem here with Louis Mac-Neice's ominous 'Prayer Before Birth' or Philip Larkin's 'Born Yesterday'. The verse form – six-line stanzas with two short lines in the middle – is finely controlled. The first verse is an invocation to the unborn child, urging it not to come into a world of suffering and apprehension. Verse two extends this idea by asserting that nothing can be changed by the coming child. Subtly we are reminded of the child who did come and who wrought change: Christ. The third verse tacitly asks the question of the child: if it knew all there was to know about life, would it accept it for what it (life) is? Verse four deals with the inevitability of the birth anyway; and verse five underlines the poet's compassion and at the same time registers his acknowledgement that man cannot change anything. Yet the final verse is optimistic in tone: the child may find 'Health, love, friends, scope' despite its start in life. In many ways this is similar to the previous poem: there the landscape contrasted with the bird's song; here the fears and sufferings of life are finally diminished in an upsurge of faith in humanity.

wombed souls i.e. those conceived but not yet born.
terrestrial chart i.e. earthly pattern of life.
locked sense i.e. because shut in the womb, unable to feel, hear, see what is outside.
pending plan i.e. what will happen.
the common lot to rare i.e. to change the common lot of mankind (suffering and unhappiness) to the rare (happiness and fulfilment).
unreasoning Relying on our belief that life will be happy rather than our reason which tells us it will not.
sanguine Hopeful, confident.

Shut out that Moon

A finely sustained cynical assertion of the changes wrought by time. The moon is traditionally associated with romance and love, but the poet chooses to reject its past associations – the outside, freedom of love and life – and to accept, or apparently accept, imprisonment in the room, which is perhaps synonymous with domesticity. It is, too, a sad lament for joys now gone. The irony is seen in the fact that this is a lyric which is sad rather than joyful. Yet there is a lightness in the verse, the running alliteration making for a kind of joy even in sadness. This is more than counterbalanced by the superb verbal usage of 'Prison'.

Before our lutes were strewn i.e. before the joys of life – the songs and dances of youth – (become dusty).
dew-dashed Fine coinage, indicating Hardy's almost casually poetic observation.
Brush not the bough Note the fine contrast employed in this stanza with the previous one – there the contemplation of the heavens, here that of nature and the past associations of love. Unobtrusive indication that the room is 'shared' – but only in person, not in spirit. Note the change in this verse from the imperative which has opened the first three.
Too tart the fruit i.e. sour.

After the Last Breath

Not the conventional death-bed scene, but a moving and constrained reaction to the aftermath of death. It is a typically individualistic treatment, and the verse form (yet another variant of the four-line stanza with a short end-stopped line at the conclusion), is handled with deft assurance. It is noteworthy that the first two verses are simply, directly expressed, while the third lists the medical trappings which were ineffectual and now have no use. The last two verses express death as a kind of freedom, as compared with life for those who live on.

list Listen.

Our morrow's anxious plans Note the ironic concept of death the great leveller as compared with the petty affairs of men, for so often we plan in vain.

its silly face Note how effective the personification is, ironically, *after* the death.

savours i.e. tastes, strictly speaking. But here 'appears' or 'seems' would perhaps be better.

by littles Unusual term meaning 'by degrees'.

Outshapes i.e. appears.

The Convergence of the Twain
(Lines on the loss of the *Titanic*)

James Gibson's commentary precludes the necessity of any introduction here, except perhaps the added note that the poem has a resonance and elevation more commonly associated with an ode.

tidal lyres i.e. the tides in their regularity of movement are compared to the strings, the rhythmic plucking of which produce melody.

grotesque, slimed Note the effect achieved by the single words, each obliquely conveying the tragedy.

What does this vaingloriousness down here? The speaking fish are a moment of bathos, rare in Hardy, who usually manages to sustain his tone.

In shadowy silent distance Note how the longer line 'grows' like the iceberg which is being described.

august Ironically used word in the light of the disaster.

At Tea

Shorter than a sonnet; yet in two halves that are rather like that form. A moment in time recaptured, with the strongly suggestive 'might have been', which, as we have seen earlier, forms an important part of Hardy's appraisal of passing situations. The verse is limpid and simple, reflecting the smooth gloss that covers the reality, the last line providing an unvoiced indication of inner feelings. Note that the couplets reveal the situation fully.

that she fills an envied place i.e. she is being complacent, secure.
abloom i.e. with excitement, perhaps in the knowledge that she is still loved; or in the knowledge of the shared secret of the past with the husband. Or perhaps she has taken particular trouble with her appearance, to outshine her married rival.
And he throws her a stray glance The unexpectedness is half the effect, the other half lying in the deception and its corollary – the future of the marriage, the unhappiness of the husband being unvoiced but felt.

By Her Aunt's Grave

Superb short poem, finely ironic, cynical (but true) in its appraisal of a kind of human nature. The irony lies in the pathetic 'respectability' of old age (which saves for a headstone and thus achieves respectability in death), as distinct from the heartlessness of youth, which spends in one evening the money saved over eighty weeks. The breaking of trust is thus thematic here, and there is the additional implication of the man influencing the girl, perhaps not merely to an abuse of trust, but towards seduction and the abuse of her too. The dialogue gives the poem a certain dramatic force and immediacy; but note the brilliantly conveyed effect in the last line, which is not in speech but in commentary.

In the Cemetery

A sonnet that is an ironic comment on human nature and the reality of death, but with a finely sympathetic penetration into the individual need to let go, to release emotion which has a focus in the loved ones who are dead. Again the use of speech provides a certain poignant force. The comment also embraces the natural tendency towards argument and underpins the possessiveness inherent in most of us.

like sprats in a tin A superb simile to define the anonymity of death, its essential sameness which, ironically, cannot be grasped by the individual mourner.

And as well cry over a new-laid drain The psychology of this is
unerring – and in addition there is the comment that we weep over
what appears, for example the grave and the flowers which symbolize
the beloved, rather than the reality which we cannot see.

The Going

This opens the sequence of poems which have reference to the
death of Emma Hardy. The technical mastery, with its poignant
variation of tone and the blending of a distant past with the
stultifying recent one is the hallmark of mature poetic
expression.

close your term here A euphemistic way of describing what the poet
finds so unacceptable – death.
ever anon i.e. presently. But note the force of 'ever'.
lip me Note the softness, almost tenderness that the word implies.
morning harden . . . Unmoved, unknowing The suggestion is that all
personal qualities possessed by the day are dead – as she is; and it is
finely descriptive as well.
Had place i.e. had taken place.
for a breath i.e. for a moment (as fleeting as a breath).
Life unrolled i.e. this was the best time of our lives.
vanishing Another euphemism for death, but emphatic of the
suddenness and completeness of the 'going'.
I seem but a dead man held on end . . . would undo me so The moving
quality of these lines is apparent – the broken phrases are as sighs or
tears; the breaking down after the sustained expression, quite
dignified; the grief; the regret for the wasted years. And perhaps the
most poignant part of this is the self-knowledge that has come with
death: the moving evidence that we do not know our innermost
thoughts or feelings until personal tragedy reveals them to us.

The Haunter

This is almost a reply to the previous poem, for in one leap of
the spectral imagination, so to speak, Hardy has written the
poem in the wished-for words of his dead wife. The eight-line
verses are a recurring pattern of rhyme, and there is a fine
fluidity about the whole poem, almost as if the essence of the
spirit has been captured and distilled in a light flow of expression. The poignancy lies in the inability to communicate between
the two worlds – that of the supposed spirit of the dead with that

of the continuing cycle of the living. The same note of regret, of time wasted in the past, is apparent throughout this poem as in the previous one.

where the past is all to him The phrase 'haunted' Hardy, and recurs with a slight variation in 'The Voice'.

O tell him The whole of this verse is really a poignant cry not only from the 'haunter', but from the poet, for reassurance of continuing love, a love not fully appreciated in life.

The Walk

Two eight-line verses, almost lyrical in tone, but imbued with that quality of wistfulness found in the last two poems. The sense of loneliness and isolation is most marked. The end of the first verse epitomizes what is taken for granted in life; while the end of the second underlines this by the expression of loss. This last line does not rise to a climax of discovery, but rather falls away in a finely expressed understatement; almost as if the poet, by speaking of the 'look of the room', is obliquely uttering what Wordsworth called 'thoughts that do often lie too deep for tears' – thus underlining the fact that Emma is *not* there, but elsewhere. Note the particular poignancy of 'Not thinking of you as left behind' in view of the fact that she is now permanently 'left behind' – dead. The simplicity of the language reflects the terrible emptiness of loss.

The Voice

This evocation of 'utter loss' is a vivid recollection, which equates with the wind the voice the poet *wants* to hear, as he stands in a desolate lonely place. The poem is written in quatrains, with a dextrous use of repetition and triple rhymes at the ends of lines, almost as if the echo of the longed-for voice has been captured. Alternate lines rhyme, but the mood is sustained by varying the flow of the verse with lines that stop abruptly in the middle, as the poet's consciousness adjusts itself to the encroachments of the past. It is superbly structured, a piece of technical virtuosity; the long-line first two verses sound the deeps of memory, while the last two short-line verses contract into the present – from the questioning third verse down to the final desolation of the poet as he stands alone in an isolated place, emotionally and mentally stripped by memory.

when our day was fair i.e. when we were happy, when fate smiled on us.
Wind oozing thin Unusual association, for 'oozing' is usually of liquid. Note the onomatopoeic quality which actually conveys the *sound* of the wind.

At Castle Boterel

Another thematic exploration of the past and its searing effect upon the present: in seven verses of five lines each, the much shorter line at the close of each verse sometimes running naturally into the next one. Again the poet looks back in time to an excursion taken with his loved one, so that the poem is a mixture of poignant nostalgia on the one hand and the deep pathos of age and acceptance on the other. The mastery of the form is shown by the confident stopping in the middle of the line where appropriate, and the sustaining of a confiding tone of conversational ease.

Something that life will not be baulked of i.e. love.
In that hill's story? A subtly transferred emphasis – the story is of the lovers' exchanges – and of many other lovers too.
the transitory in Earth's long order i.e. what passes in life, involving change.
for my sand is sinking A poignant recognition of age, that he has not long to live, the metaphor being that of the sand in the hour-glass.

After a Journey

This is written in four eight-line verses; the theme of a return to the past being given a like actuality to that of the previous poem. The revisit to a place where love and happiness were enjoyed is another expression of constancy, since the final lines assert that

> I am just the same as when
> Our days were a joy, and our paths through flowers.

There is the customary running alliteration and repetition; fine natural observation; the use of archaic and dialect words to stress the past and concrete reality: the recognizable hall-marks of Hardy's manner at the time. Once again we are aware of that unique sense of recall across the years, resulting in the evocation at will of physical description, scene and atmosphere.

twain Two of us.
Time's derision i.e. the mocking laughter because of what they 'wasted'.
mist-bow The spectrum that forms above the spray. Note how cleverly Hardy uses repetition here, the poignant emphasis of 'then'.
flitting Passing lightly, i.e. like a ghost!
the stars close their shutters Effective domestic metaphor applied contrastingly, as it were, to the house of the heavens.
lours Is dark and threatening.

Beeny Cliff
(March 1870–March 1913)

Written in triplets with an insistent rhythm, initially capturing the joyfulness of youth and finally the grandeur of the scene despite the death of the loved one. In terms of sheer richness of colour, depth of association and verbal virtuosity, this poem bears comparison with anything that Hardy ever wrote.

loyally loved me This seems to imply an inequality between them which Hardy remembers, that she loved him *despite* . . . It reflects how carefully the words are weighed here.
ceaseless babbling Note how the last word conveys the sounds of the mews.
A little cloud . . . And the Atlantic dyed its levels . . . misfeatured Almost a prophetic symbol, the 'clear-sunned' reflecting their love, the above references the obscuring of it in their life, and the next line – 'And then the sun burst out . . .' the re-kindling of that love for him later.
balks Note the fine onomatopoeic effect.
And nor knows nor cares for Beeny Certainly nature is permanent and the life of man ephemeral, but here what is unsaid is as important as what is said – she cannot know or care for the writer either. Note how 'laugh' brilliantly picks up the 'laughed' of line 6.

The Frozen Greenhouse
(St Juliot)

Finely economical poem in short-line verses, again recalling an incident and linking it unequivocally with the present; the changed circumstances; the ironic survival of a thing (the greenhouse) as against the death of the loved one. It is a small sad song, none the less effective because the lilting regret is conveyed with exactitude, and balanced in past and present with an exquisite attention to contrasting details – note that the greenhouse is 'Warm, tight, and gay' while the plants were 'Cold, iced, forgot' – and that both phrases apply equally to the dead woman, in her life and in her death.

On a Discovered Curl of Hair

Another effective simple poem, again evocative of the past and its relation to the present. This time it is written in couplets, with some unusual choices of words and the now familiar balance between the past and the present struck in the two halves of the poem.

dinned Were noisy, but note the onomatopoeic quality of the word.
absentness Fine choice, conveying much more than 'absence', for the length of the word itself looks forward to the 'absentness' that is now permanent for the poet.
For brightest brown have donned a grey i.e. she was grey-haired before she died.
Beams with live brown The word 'live' is the important one, contrasting immediately with the fact of death.

A Night in November

There is a fine imaginative connection between the suffering of man and the suffering of nature in this poem of three quatrains with alternate lines rhyming. The first verse describes the out-side tumult of the storm; in the second the tree symbolizes the loss of man; while the third (in which the man touches what the tree has lost – the leaf – and imagines that it is his loved one), brings man into empathy with nature. The result is a poem of succinct identification of mood and atmosphere.

a tree declared to the gloom Personification, but the outside wailing and shaking of the tree – its language if you like – can be imagined.
And saying at last you knew i.e. that he still loved her.

During Wind and Rain

The poem exerts a powerful effect through the associations of memory: each of the four verses having a refrain which takes the form of a lament for the passage of time, the passing of youth and life and the inevitable onset of death. At the end of the poem we realize that the names on the gravestones have moved the poet to journey into the past, for the poem, while focusing on more than one, always has the one – the dead beloved – in mind.

Mooning This is one of the many fine visual effects.
the white storm-birds wing across Just as birds presage a storm, so Hardy uses the image to suggest change and, ultimately, death.
And the rotten rose is ript from the wall Death comes to all things, and the description anticipates the removal of the furniture and fittings when the owners are dead. The power is in the word 'ript'.
Down their carved names This is a reference to the gravestones which mark the final resting place of those described in the poem.

Channel Firing

The student should familiarize himself with the fact that the supposed narrator is a dead man, and carefully read James Gibson's commentary.

altar-crumb i.e. the mouse stealing the consecrated bread.
blow the trumpet i.e. to summon the dead to judgement.

In Time of 'The Breaking of Nations'

This much-anthologized piece, written in quatrains with alternate lines rhyming, has a timeless universality. It contemplates the tragedy of the First World War, and its theme is quite simply the unchanging nature of the simple things of life – reflected in an agricultural landscape – as distinct from the rise and fall of kingdoms and empires. The tone is wry, ironic, yet imbued with compassion; it throws into sardonic and uncompromising relief the passing glory and pointlessness of war. The last verse conveys a perfect perspective: after the hate of nations has ravaged, the simple individual existence, permanence and love will continue and outlast all such mammoth struggles.

annals Historical records, narrative of events year by year.

Ten Years Since

A very simple poetic exercise, but showing amazing facility in rhyming and rhythmic ability for a man of eighty-two. Despite the lightness of touch the regret comes through as the positive motivation behind a poem which is pleasant both to the ear and to the eye. It reflects Hardy's ability not only to fashion out of memory the importance of loss, but also to make poetry out of the simple domestic occurrences that are the major part of life.

Nobody Comes

Another poem written in old age. It shows a remarkably keen observation, particularly in the description of the telegraph wire. And the repetition of the word 'spectral' shows that Hardy himself is still haunted by the past. Although this was written well after his second marriage, the sense of isolation, of being cut off from the experience of life, is very apparent in the final lines of the poem. The telegraph and the car have come into the land, but the effect of something coming and going means the negation of humanity, of what is permanent, perhaps, in country tradition. Although telegraph wires provide a means of communication, the sight of them on a lonely road seems to emphasize our own sense of isolation.

Intones to travellers like a spectral lyre Note how Hardy's ear has caught keenly the actual noise of the wires.
whangs Again an accurate, onomatopoeic effect is produced.
mute Conveys simply the lack of communication between man and the man-made: the wire and the car.

Night in the Old Home

Again the haunting of the past, this time the many ancestors instead of the 'woman much missed'. The long lines of the verses reflect the length of life and the backward-looking area spanned by memory. The theme is quite clearly a sense of his own difference from his ancestors, in the sense that they took life as it came, whereas he has questioned it and has expressed his doubts. The last verse is particularly effective, with the single words, in two batches of three, defining the ancestral view.

My perished people i.e. those from the distant past, the dead.
A pale late plant A reflection of his age: their 'final' descendant.
which consigns men to night A reference to his own cynicism.
fevered i.e. we did not fret and worry over things that did not concern us.

A Private Man on Public Men

A poetic exercise in the assumed voice of the man who has withdrawn from public life, written in the comparatively unusual form for Hardy of the rhyming couplet.

the Senate Parliament.

The Superseded

This poem focuses as Hardy so often does, on what is a commonplace: the feeling in age that younger people have overtaken and passed you despite your own feeling that you can continue and have much to offer. There is a note of bitterness in the first two verses, but this gives way to regret, a regret that is ironic in view of what Hardy was still to achieve in verse. It is an uneven poem, balanced between the pathos of old age and the bathos of repetition.

unforetold A typical Hardy use of the negative, which here echoes the negation of being 'superseded'.

He Never Expected Much
(or) A Consideration (*A reflection*) on my eighty-sixth birthday

The consideration is once more a looking-back to childhood, and a pondering on the lessons life taught him then. The 'neutral-tinted haps' are a kind of learning to live with happiness and suffering and preparing yourself to do so. This is what the poet feels he has learned, and what he has lived by. Note the repetition of the refrain, a favourite Hardy device.

stem Bear.
assign i.e. give to me.

'I Look Into My Glass'

Another superbly condensed poem, which describes the ageing of the body and yet the capacity of the heart to experience suffering as keenly as ever. It is beautifully balanced, beginning with the look in the mirror that reflects the 'wasting skin', this linking immediately with the expression of loneliness in the second verse (a reflection in a mirror is hardly companionship). The third verse asserts that Time 'part steals, lets part abide': in other words takes away the physical but leaves the emotional. In a small way this is a bold poem, enunciating what is an inviolable truth about the nature of age, with a wistful recognition that has a certain moving dignity. Note too the use of 'Would God'. Speech, as we have seen, often gives dramatic immediacy to a Hardy poem.

endless rest i.e. death.

Afterwards

The poet here effects to foresee the aftermath of his own death, with his idea of what people will say, for example, of his attitude towards nature. The five quatrains, with alternate lines rhyming, have a sonorous effect, almost funereal in atmosphere and emphasis. There are some fine individual coinages by Hardy, together with minute observation and sense-awareness. Alliteration is heavy, as befits the mournful nature of the subject. There is, too, an undercurrent of wry recognition, perhaps best exemplified in the unanswered question at the end of three of the verses. The poem tells us much of Hardy the man.

tremulous The word conveys at once the idea of age and the temporary nature of life itself.
like wings/Delicate-filmed as new-spun silk Fine simile and epithets, which indicate the subtle beauty of the veins on a leaf.
eyelid's soundless blink/The dewfall hawk Again the minute observation, and the linking of movement in man and nature.
wind-warped Alliterative epithet which describes how the wind 'bends' the thorn bushes.

furtively Note the pathos of the word – the hedgehog can only travel safely in the dark.

stilled Another euphemism for death.

full-starred heavens . . . this thought rise Notice the description of the fullness of life in the universe, and the subtle idea of a thought that 'rises' – like the moon. This kind of association is part of the imaginative structure of the poem.

outrollings A fine choice of word which captures the echo of the bell.

Revision questions on Poems mainly autobiographical

1 Write an essay on Hardy's use of the past and the present in any *two* of the poems in this section.

2 Indicate the part played by nature in interaction with personal relationships in any *two* or *three* of Hardy's poems.

3 Write an account of any *theme* present in Hardy's poems in this section, and show how he presents it.

4 In what ways is nostalgia an important element in Hardy's poetry? You should quote from a number of poems in support of your views.

5 Consider Hardy's use of two or more verse forms, and write an essay of appreciation, saying how they affect his treatment of the subject about which he is writing.

6 Write an appreciation of any two poems that deal with childhood in this section.

7 Discuss Hardy's use of irony in any two or three poems here.

8 Show how Hardy presents commonplace moments or incidents in his verse. You should refer to two or more poems in your answer.

9 Write an essay on Hardy's treatment of the 'might-have-been' in his verse.

10 In what way do you find Hardy's poetry cynical? *or* Write an essay on 'loving-kindness' in his verse.

11 Write a detailed analysis of any *two* poems which deal with the death of Hardy's first wife.

Incidents and stories

The Pine Planters
(Marty South's reverie)

A fine lyrical poem in four-line verse in the first section and twelve-line stanzas in the second, though in effect they share the same length of line and rhythmic regularity. The first part is an imaginative identification of Marty South's love for Giles Winterborne. The first publication of the poem (in 1903) made no mention of Marty; the second section deals with a strong empathy between man (or woman here) and nature, an identification which, it must be stressed, runs throughout *The Woodlanders* (1887), at least in the characters of Giles and Marty. The first section of 'The Pine Planters' is a controlled inward monologue, its main burden being one person's lack of awareness of the other, although they are working together in close proximity. As we have seen in the previous poems, this theme has been fully orchestrated by Hardy on a personal domestic level. The second section here deals with the planting of a tree and its developing of a 'voice' – the imaginative implication being that we, and nature, grow up into suffering. The fullness of the identification is ironic: the tree cannot move or speak; it can only endure. There is a fine alliterative 'song' throughout; and the poem gives the impression of being astutely balanced: a comment on life and love, with a final aside on old age too. The personification of the tree is undertaken in the language of studied understatement; suffering is the lot of man and nature, both being exposed to the 'storms' of life.

welter Rolling, hurly-burly.
halt Lamed, crippled.

Tess's Lament

Another poem of sadness in love, and again derived from the situation in one of his own novels, here the speaker being the heroine of *Tess of the d'Urbervilles* (1891). The metrical treatment is very important, for the repetition, running into the second line, conveys the rocking motion to which Gosse refers, almost as if the speaker is swaying to and fro in the anguish of utterance. The 'lament' is in character, for Tess's capacity to blame herself is part of that fullness of nature which makes her baptize her child Sorrow on the one hand and kill her lover Alec d'Urberville on the other. The readers of the novel will recall the physical and emotional shock of her being hanged, and this gives to the poem a consciously ironic element. The poignancy and the desolation are finely conveyed in the simple, insistent expression.

And no more see the sun Ironically, this is to be her 'lot'.

nook Secluded place.

within the chimney-seat Very ironically used here, since Tess even then sat out of the light, secluded (see 'nook' above) but was 'found out' (just as her past is 'found out' later).

The flowers we potted Note the immediate parallel with nature – the dead flowers, the 'dead' love.

dock Coarse, weedy herb.

it was I who did it all For readers of the novel, the irony once more – Tess is blameless in the true sense of the word.

guile Deception.

my cross Tess is, in effect, a martyr.

my fate as writ i.e. as laid down.

unbe Fine use of the negative involving irony – Tess is really saying that she wishes she had not lived her past life.

Boys Then and Now

A brief but telling song of innocence and experience. It captures, in four simple verses, that area of childhood belief in something which adulthood proved was false, and yet there remains to the man who was a child the innocence and the treasuring of that belief. The poem goes further, for the changes between the generations, the recognition of what has come to be called the 'generation gap' is implicit in the poem: it is a wise and simple assertion of an inviolable truth.

new trim i.e. fresh blossom.

old already A cynical record of what can often be the case: the son who knows more than, and is already superior to, his father.

At the Railway Station, Upway

Hardy is adept, as we have seen, at making poetry out of a moment that is either commonplace or grotesque or, as here, poignant. We don't even know if the little boy is the son of the convict, or whether he is trying to earn money by playing at being 'imprisoned' himself in poverty; or whether it is a moment of childish compassion for the man about to go to prison, an outward movement of the heart to shame the grown-ups. Strangely, it doesn't matter, for the whole scene is depicted with an ironic wry understanding that immediately registers with the reader. It is a small incident of human contact, the compassion and participation transcending the inherent sadness. Note the variation of the rhyme-scheme and lengths of line within the poem to register mood and music.

pitying Unusual form of the word, exactly conveying here the motivation of the little boy.
grimful glee Almost a paradox, but exactly showing the man's ironic appraisal of his own situation.

In a Waiting Room

Hardy was fascinated by the casual encounter, often making a minute observation of it and its significance in the broader perspective of life. Once again the scene is set before a journey. The poem encompasses the changes in mood we experience as casual events affect us, and the verse form is adjusted to fit this. The movement of the poem is an outward one, from the bag-man's calculations in the Bible to the real-life experience of the soldier and his wife, perhaps for ever parting – the burden of adult life – and to the children's responses to what the writer had regarded as 'fly-blown'. This movement is from pessimism to optimism, to a faith in youth and its innocent delight as distinct from the worries of age. There is a strong Romantic attitude here towards youth and innocence. As ever, the use of speech adds to the immediacy.

suchwise bent An economical way of saying 'if they were so inclined'.
cypher i.e. calculate.
charmless scene Note the irony – the apathy – successfully conveyed by this choice of word.

A smear of tragedy The image connects with 'fly-blown': lives are tainted too.

Subdued to stone by strong endeavour Notice how the metaphor conveys the smooth surface of self-control over their inward suffering.

It rained on the skylight Note how the outside world contrasts with the sudden 'glory' spread by the children's joy in life.

The Bird-catcher's Boy

Fine ballad, the first part in the form of dialogue, and again a distinct underlining of the generation gap. Briefly, the boy objects to his father's way of earning a living, escapes from the 'cage' of home – from which the birds can't escape – and, on the night he is drowned, appears to return to touch the wires of the bird-cages, just as he had done before he left. Hardy is the master of such narrative – simple, poignant, humane *and* with narrative tension and dramatic effects: we want to know what happened. One of the major facets of Hardy's art is his ability to tell a story, whether it be in verse or prose, and here we find all the compassion of the boy and the anguish of the parents who have lost him. There is also a social and moral comment implicit in the two attitudes, that of father and son, towards the imprisoning of the birds; and we know that Hardy's sympathies lie beyond the job-necessity of the man. The irony lies in the fact that the boy has run away to sea but has been wrecked – just as the birds he loved are wrecked by imprisonment. The ballad is imbued with Hardy's sense of a malign fate which 'wrecks' the innocent.

dolt Fool.

pat Properly.

Lightless An uncommon word, here carrying a moral weight as well.

caged choirs i.e. captured birds. Note that the musical image is echoed in the boy's action, an underlining of his sympathy with the birds – it is almost a caress.

wist Knew.

groping touch Note the effect of this word – conveying uncertainty – as distinct from the 'harp-like' touch of the boy when alive.

much Again the economical usage, here meaning 'much as if'.

A Wife Waits

Another short realistic capturing of a situation and an immediate imaginative and sympathetic identification with the speaker. The theme is the sudden cooling of love, the man returning to his old haunts. The comment embraces a sardonic look at marriages that are made in romance and die at the touch of reality: almost a poignant comment on Hardy's own marriage. It is a ballad, only three verses being needed to tell the story. There is even a sadness in the idea of the woman's constancy.

treading a tune i.e. dancing.
Dear The capitalization reinforces the irony of her situation – she is no longer 'dear' but has been reduced to waiting on her man.
shivering Notice how effective this word is, emphasized by the rhythmic fall at the beginning of the line.

The Market-girl

Subtle variation in the two verses here, for the second incorporates an internal rhyme and the longer lines reflect the building of the relationship after the initial question. Again it is a commonplace enough situation, but here with the dressing of romance, not autobiographical of course, though the man does speak and his courtship begins. The might-have-been is translated into reality. The long lines of each verse are in rhyming couplets.

Throwing a Tree
(New Forest)

The four-line verses here are so handled that the longer fourth lines firstly presage the fall of the tree, then describe it, and reflect the long-drawn-out efforts of the men, as well as the time of the growing and falling that Hardy is so careful to stress. The identification with nature is so sympathetic that the actions of the men are *felt*, and what is a job becomes an event of importance. Both the technique and the contrast inherent in the poem might be studied by looking back at 'The Pine Planters' and comparing it with this poem. It would reveal Hardy's meticulous attention to the details of his verse forms and rhythms, even to the point of sound and movement.

axes Meant to remind us of historic executions.

the proud tree that bears the death-mark i.e. has been marked for 'execution', like so many diseased elms suffering from Dutch elm disease in our own time.

lie white on the moss There is a certain purity about the image, as if this is the 'blood' of a great independent virginal being.

gash Powerfully evocative of pain and suffering.

The saw then begins Notice how this verse, with its shorter lines initially, reflects the cutting movement.

the living mast Hardy is not unmindful of the associations with ships, and the word 'living' is particularly effective by way of stressing the contrast.

Job and Ike The two 'executioners'. It is almost as if they shudder at the destruction and the knowledge that their turn will come.

two hundred years . . . two hours As we have seen, Hardy employs contrast, but with a telling humanity here; for history, tradition – two of Hardy's major themes – are broken in nature, which has the greatest history and tradition of all.

The Old Workman

The four-line verses have two rhyming lines, but the second pair is rounded off with a shorter end-stopped line. The poem contains some pathos on account of the injuries suffered by the workman, but there is a certain exalted tone as his pride in what he has achieved – for others – is described. Again, the poem begins as a dialogue, but settles into the one speaker's account. As few writers before him, Hardy was obviously conscious of the dignity of labour.

crookt i.e. bent.

walled from wind and rain The contrast is immediately apparent – the mason has spent his life unprotected from the elements, but what he builds is a protection for others.

They don't know me . . . When I lie underground Apart from the sentiment of pride in one's work, there is also the moral implication that working to do good for others is the standard to live by. What is ironic is the lack of contact between the mason and the people he has built for – a lack of contact which we are aware of and dismiss, but which Hardy chooses to emphasize in this passing comment on life.

The Choirmaster's Burial

This is a further instance of Hardy's versatility in the use of form, for the lines are short and the rhymes are picked up almost like notes in music – an indication of the poet's achieving some degree of harmony with his subject. There is thus, though we are dealing with death, a lightness of touch – rather as if the ghostly choirmaster of the poem is himself conducting. This ghostly effect is at times tantalizing, but the theme of the poem is quite clearly the exercise of human response to a request. This contrasts with the practice of the Vicar, for he merely follows the ritual of Christian observance despite the known wish of the dead man.

task us i.e. be too much for us.
grave-brim Graveside, but unusually put.
To get through it faster A damning comment on the Vicar's Christianity.
Like the saints in church-glass Comparing the essential 'earthly' or 'ghostly' saints with those who have a permanent place. There is also contrast with the Vicar.

The Sacrilege
(A Ballad-tragedy. About 182–)

A ballad divided into two parts, and only with the opening of Part 2 do we realize that the narrator is dead, and that the whole is informed therefore with a mysterious and macabre atmosphere. The story is quite straightforward: a man who robs a church for his mistress is caught in the act. Before he is hanged he places upon his brother the burden of revenge: should his rival, Wrestler Joe, take over his mistress, then the brother is to kill her. The narrative is brilliantly sustained, rich in local atmosphere and colour, with a running repetition of the landmarks throughout. Places visited, dialect echoes, visual pictures and a mastery of dialogue all play their part in what is essentially a dramatic narrative. Mention has been made earlier of Hardy's story-telling ability; and this poem and the three following ones – in which the horrible, the pathetic, the tragic and the supernatural all play a part – are testimony to that ability. One sees here Hardy's working of the mines of folklore and legend; with an awareness of his own roots, those of the hearth, the fireside with the stories of the elders. Perhaps the greatest common factor of appeal in each of these poems is the dramatic immediacy Hardy achieves through the simple recital – in each case the teller of the tale is intimately involved in the action, and the reader shares fears, hopes, even actions and reactions. In the first poem the verses are of eight lines, with a repeated word as rhyme in the first and third, and a triple rhyme in the second half of each verse. Personification – for instance of Dunkery – and alliteration abound throughout.

gallanting The *English Dialect Dictionary* gives this as 'gay, roving, roaming', but the implication is 'keeping company with, courting'.

Dunkery frowns This is repeated, and is a natural, ominous symbol, as if they are fated.

swift sweets outwore i.e. the happy times passed.

beauties bright as tulips blown i.e. her lips.

van i.e. caravan.

sloe-black Sudden economical coinage: black sloes are ripe, and give added depth (and temptation) to her eyes.

dallyings i.e. flirtation.

finger Steal.

mart Market.

I've stayed my hand i.e. I have drawn the line, refused to steal.

Curbed by a law not of the land i.e. superstitious fear.

pouts Note the immediate connection with nature.

my soul's imperilling i.e. that I shall go to hell.

who is my ravishing i.e. seduces me by her charm.

botchery . . . assay Making a mess of . . . this rash attempt.

bedwinner Fine coinage, an obvious verbal echo of the common 'breadwinner'.

Born at my birth i.e. his twin.

Or one more foul i.e. his evil spirit.

ill-witchery . . . lure of eyes There is a sexual and a supernatural implication here.

And yet I could not bear i.e. to do what he had been asked to do.

figure i.e. appear.

clave . . . cleaves i.e. the natural association again. The word means 'stuck fast to'.

Your goodman's The implication of the brother is that Wrestler Joe may have drowned.

such might bode What it meant.

undue i.e. untimely.

He sees . . . Until his judgement-time There is a compulsive guilt about this, somewhat reminiscent of the Ancient Mariner's in Coleridge's poem of that name.

A Trampwoman's Tragedy
(182–)

Again the story in outline is a simple one; two wandering couples, with the narrator flirting with the other man and in a rash moment falsely admitting that he is the father of her coming child. Her lover thereupon kills the man, is hanged for it; and the woman (having had a still-born child), sees her lover's ghost. Thereafter it is she who continues to haunt the Western Moor. The eight-line verse is employed, but with the variant of a short second line, and a similar use of repetition as a refrain. This adds substantially to the building up of an emotional atmosphere. Hardy is very good at conveying primitive passion and impulsiveness in these ballad stories.

turnpike tracks Presumably following the old road, which would have a toll-gate on it for the payment of a tax.
landskip sights i.e. (the best) view: in this case the inn.
O deadly day i.e. an ill-fated one.
at last we won i.e. climbed.
and Mother Lee/Passed to my former one An early form of itinerant wife-swapping, or mistress-swapping, as the case may be.
Gilded . . . glazing Note the colour and the heavy alliteration, which reflect the deed.
swung i.e. was hanged.
stained i.e. he had only one other crime: the stealing of a horse when he needed it.
death-day . . . dead-born Note the effectiveness of the repetition, and the macabre, supernatural coincidence implied.
and thinned away The words convey the ghostly 'fading'.

A Sunday Morning Tragedy
(about 186–)

This time the poem is in a straightforward ballad form with alternate lines rhyming, and the narrator is the mother of the tragic heroine of the tale. Finding her daughter pregnant, she pleads with the man to marry her and, on his refusal to do so, the mother consults a shepherd about a herbal method of abortion. She tries it and then, when her daughter is taken ill, finds that the lover is prepared to marry the girl after all. They find the girl dead when they go to see her.

flower-fair Simple epithet, later to be ironically echoed in 'picotee'.
joyed Note the unusual, rhythmically fitting verbal usage.
plodded . . . pleaded Part of the running alliteraton used by Hardy.
to sail the main i.e. go to sea.
Though better I had ceased It would have been better if I had not done so.
'Or none?' A pathetic indication that the mother knows she is doing wrong – hoping for an answer that will tell her there is no herb that can bring about the abortion.
The sunset-shine Brilliantly ironic, since the shepherd, normally associated with good, is here the bringer of evil.
baulk i.e. prevent.
Why should they be? The question is again indicative of the mother's unhappiness at going against nature by using the herb, but the voice is Hardy's own.
poppling Tossing, rippling.
wind whiffled wailfully i.e. nature is already mourning the coming deed: 'whiffled' means slight movements of air or wind.
lours Scowls, frowns.
fond salute i.e. loving greeting.
betimes Early.
raiment . . . sackcloth-clad Note the immediate contrast: the outward showing-off at church; and the garments of penitence.
bantered Joked, teased.
Death had took her . . . Death took not me Note the effective contrast: the living suffer on.
colding A fine word to indicate the onset of death, the gradual disappearance of life.
not **to pity me** Her sense of guilt and remorse is such that she does not want to be pardoned by God. The tragedy is as much hers as her daughter's.

The Lost Pyx
(A Medieval Legend)

In this poem, which covers the areas of the Christian and the supernatural, Hardy makes great use of internal rhyme and an insistent rhythm. Although the legend has another less pleasant version, the one given here sounds, for a change, a note of optimism. One night a priest hears a call telling him to go and shrive a man who is dying. He ignores it at first, but after seeing a visage frowning down on him from Heaven, he sets out through the terrible night only to find, when he arrives at the home of the dying man, that the pyx containing the Holy Sacrament is missing. He turns back on his tracks and finds the pyx on a hill, surrounded by all the worshipping animals of nature. The priest returns to the cottage, where he kneels in prayer, and gives the last rites to the dying man. Later, he has a stone raised in memory of the occasion.

Alternate rhymes and half rhymes abound, and long lines also alternate with shorter and more emphatic ones. The use of dialogue provides a dramatic and insistent narrative.

Attests i.e. bears witness to.

trees twanged We have seen that Hardy is greatly observant of the noise and movement of the trees, and the onomatopoeic effect here reflects the stormy night.

in hail i.e. within calling distance.

And head in a heat of shame Superbly simple, economical description to underline his feelings.

freight i.e. the Pyx.

won place i.e. become the sub-prior.

Revision questions on Incidents and stories

1 Compare and contrast any *two* of the longer poems in this section, bringing out clearly Hardy's story-telling ability and the verse techniques he uses.

2 By a study of any *two* or *three* poems in this section, show how Hardy makes poetry out of a moment or an incident.

3 Write an essay on Hardy's use of *pathos* in any selection of poems from this group, and say whether or not you find his work moving.

4 Write a considered appreciation of Hardy's use of nature in any *three* of the poems in this section.

5 In what ways do the poems in this section reflect Hardy's compassion and humanity? You may refer to any three or four poems in your answer.

6 Write an essay on the variety of *form* used by Hardy in *either* the shorter *or* the longer poems in this section.

Descriptive and animal poems

Weathers

This poem of two verses – the eight lines of the narrative poems being extended here to nine – has three effective short lines to six longer ones evocative of the contrasting weather. It is full of natural observation and a direct appraisal of the way our moods are conditioned by the weather, the refrain linking the poet with the reactions of common humanity, thus giving to the verse the 'universality' which has been noted as one of the major achievements of Hardy's mature art. The interlocking rhymes common to both stanzas emphasize Hardy's concept of the unity of nature.

betumble Poetic word for 'set them falling'.
nestlings i.e. young birds just capable of flying.
little brown nightingale Note the effect of this description: the small simplicity of the bird contrasted with the beauty of the song. Think back to *The Darkling Thrush*.
And rooks in families Note the identification of man with nature yet again.

Before and After Summer

A simple and economically expressed poem in a conversational tone, written in couplets varied by alternate-line rhyming, marking clearly the passage of time in retrospect, but noting, with an ironic self-awareness, that summer has gone – and passed unnoticed at the time. The universal truth is that what we look forward to for so long passes almost before we are aware of it.

wintry scourgings i.e. the sufferings brought by winter.
a half-transparent blind The implication is that the sun will emerge, but the idea of the blind seems to convey also the fact that we hide behind the 'blinds' of our houses in bad weather.
Blank as I am even is he Once more the identification of man with nature, the inverted word order reflecting the lack of animation.

I, alas, perceived not when There is a poignant sense of time lost in this last line.

A Backward Spring

Here the emphatic mood is stressed by an account of the late arrival of spring, and the poem is built on an intimate personification seen in the reactions of nature to this arresting of the cycle. The personal qualities – fear, timidity, worry – are transferred to the trees, grass and bushes, and the second half of the poem focuses on the myrtle, the final lines going back to its survival in the winter. Again the alternate-line rhyming is varied by couplets and shorter lines.

And the primrose pants Note the sense of 'pace' in nature and hence the importance of time in its due season.
Though the myrtle asks The shrub with shiny evergreen leaves and the white flowers to which Hardy refers as 'buttons'.

'If It's Ever Spring Again'
(Song)

A lyric evocative of romance and the past, the two seasons of the year, summer and spring, that are associated with love and with the stirring and movement of nature. The refrain gives an intentional lightness of touch. The references to love ('Standing with my arm around her') are nostalgic and sentimental, and there is a wistful air about the poem: a song written for singers in chorus rather than there being any personal involvement. This, however, does not detract from its lilting charm.

amid their flounder i.e. as they are floundering about.
the cuckoos-two-in-rhyme They symbolize romantic love.
achime i.e. in harmony.

An Unkindly May

Just as Hardy is the recorder of the commonplace moment, with an elevation of his own that turns it into poetry, so he is the recorder of the commonplace in nature, but with a rare eye for detail. The fact that this is an 'unkindly May' is shown in the metrical heaviness of the lines, which are thus consonant with a mood that would normally be much brighter and lighter. The whole has the effect of a painting, the rhyming couplets providing the structural frame.

blurting boisterous-wise Heavy alliteration to emphasize the scene.
like rusty cranes The simile conveys the 'unkindliness' of the month, the man-made parallel emphasizing it in view of Hardy's known affection for things natural rather than for man's mechanical trappings.
eye-trying flaps i.e. because the sudden shafts of sunlight are only occasionally seen in passing.
commendable i.e. not worthy of praise (while you are in this state).
That shepherd still stands Again the view of man against the landscape, the unchanging nature of rustic habit and time.

An August Midnight

Two simple six-line verses, consisting of a quatrain with two alternate lines rhyming and a couplet in each verse, in which the poet contemplates insect-life – its knowledge, its lore, its ritual – with its store of experience of which he can know nothing. It is a strangely moving poem, as small and complete in its compass as is the insect life described.

that rubs its hands The personification here indicates Hardy's minute observation of habit, and invests the unprotected creature with a certain pathos.
They know Earth-secrets The term is capitalized and hyphenated in order to show the largeness (to itself) of the world of the 'humblest': each creature, however small, leads a life unknown to man.

Shortening Days at the Homestead

The early Autumn days are captured here in fourteen lines – though not a sonnet – of varying line-length and a fine figurative flow. The second part opens with a question which has all the expectancy of a time loved particularly for its associations – the cider season, redolent of excitement and picking, has arrived.

The first fire since the summer Note the length of the line, equivalent to the slow rising of smoke after the long summer.

Sparrows spurt Alliterative effect that conveys the speed of movement.
whom misgivings appal i.e. they are apprehensive, for the autumn
   signals the coming return of winter – they having thought that winter
   had gone for ever. One of Hardy's imaginative associations.
Like shock-headed urchins, spiny-haired A fine image, again linking
   man and nature in an unexpected way.
pondering pace Again the alliteration reflects the movement – the slow
   tread.
embossed i.e. standing out (he is white-headed).
mill i.e. for grinding the apples, an old-fashioned liquidizer.

The Later Autumn

Three verses, again showing human and detailed observation of
nature at a certain time of the year. The short lines contrast with
the longer ones, and there is a lightness of touch despite the
season of the year, almost as if the poet delights in recording what
he sees. There is only one sombre note, which is struck at the end
of the second verse where the shades are compared to 'lives soon
to end'.

the line of your track i.e. your direction.
Leg-laden i.e. because they are loaded with pollen.
Spinning leaves . . . On whose corpses The fine personification conveys
   the life-cycle of nature, the irony of death being apparent: for the
   'scorners' are already falling.
A robin looks on An almost optimistic hint of the coming of winter.

Last Week in October

This opens with a fine personification of the trees 'undressing',
and then sharpens down to focus on the spider's web – another
manifestation in small and deadly compass. Again the contrast in
the appearance and practice of nature is central to the effects
achieved by the poet.

radiant robes This is redolent of the colours of autumn.
Here, there Note the repetition in this line – a reflection of the
   movement of the leaves.
Like a suspended criminal hangs he The image is one that strongly
   influenced Hardy who, as a child, witnessed a hanging from a distance.
as fearing a fate The unobtrusive personification of the leaves shows
   Hardy's ever-present idea of the *living* quality of nature.

The Last Chrysanthemum

These perennials can bloom into December. The verses – quatrains – are lyrically balanced, but the contemplation of this
small aspect of nature is enhanced by a strongly spiritual
ending that is almost pantheistic in its emphasis. It is a mature,
consummately planned poem, the small and great encom-
passed in its tone and in its seeing into the 'hidden harmony' of
things.

flower . . . tombs Note at once the contrast – life and death – which so
   often occurs in Hardy's verse.
leaves like corpses See the note above, for this lyric is also funereal. 'In
   the midst of life we are in death' applies to the natural cycle as well as
   to that of man.
season's shine There is much alliteration in this poem, and it makes
   for a kind of music.
witlessness The three-syllabled word conveys vacancy, a lack of
   thought.
stay its stress Delay its trials, hardships.
one mask . . . the Great Face An acknowledgement of an omniscient
   Being, the inscrutable mystery behind all things.

Winter Night in Woodland
(Old Time)

Four six-line verses which move from nocturnal activity in
nature to the bird-baiters and poachers; then to the 'land-
carriers' employed by the smugglers; and finally to the choir.
The names will be familiar to readers of Hardy's novel *Under
the Greenwood Tree*.

As from teachings of years i.e. the result of his experiences, and of the
   experiences of the fox family.
death-halloo Hardy is binding the cry of the fox-hunters to that of the
   fox hunted down and killed.
worn carols i.e. timeworn, used through the generations.
they home Another elliptical construction, eliminating 'go'.

Ice on the Highway

A human, even humorous, moment: a particular experience
captured and set down with a fine awareness of the atmosphere

but not neglecting the women's need to buy food. The verse 'slips' into lines consonant with the physical uncertainty of the conditions. There is a good sense of the give-and-take of the enforced companionship.

stagger Note also the 'staggering' rhythm of this poem.

Snow in the Suburbs

Description of a scene, the interesting treatment consisting of selective detail and control of a rhythm exactly reflecting, for example, the wayward movement of the snowflakes. This control is extended to the heavier movement of snow which nearly entombs a sparrow; then there is a finely controlled ending, attenuated lines that correspond to the size and movement of the cat. Note the effortless double rhymes in the first verse.

like a white web-foot Fine natural association, showing Hardy's keen eye.
Some flakes have lost their way The longer lines reflect the desultory movement of the flakes.
glued together like a wall This accurately defines in terms of texture the icy hardness, impenetrability, of the conditions. It is, too, a powerful tactile image.
the fleecy fall Again an appropriate association, since thick snow provides warmth, as does the wool of the sheep.
And overturns him All things in nature are relative – the 'lump', small to us, is mountainous to the sparrow.
nether Lower.
Starts off a volley Notice how the rhythm of the line captures the movement of the snow.
And we take him in As often with Hardy, the essentially human element is included: the sparrow survives, and the cat must too, here with the aid of man.

To a Tree in London
(Clement's Inn)

Short lines in triplets, sounding a pathetic note since the tree never lives among its kind but among the streets and buildings that are not its natural companions. The roots of the tree are compared to the movable roots of man; and the effect conveyed, for once in Hardy, is of a deprivation in nature.

Smoke like earth An ironic way of describing the dirty air.
a blue immense i.e. suggestive of freedom.

The Fallow Deer at the Lonely House

This superb little poem sharply focuses on the lack of correspondence between the conditions of beast and man: the latter within, in comfort, the former without, perhaps lonely. It is a moment of magical imagination, the concept going beyond sentiment because of the fine discrimination in choice of words; the single associations of the last two lines being particularly effective in setting up in the reader's consciousness a sympathetic bond with the subject of the poem. Nowhere is Hardy's humanitarian concern for animals and his imaginative identification with their state seen to better advantage. The poem is as finely structured as a lovingly created building, as beautiful in symmetry as the deer itself.

discern Stronger than 'see', because the eye of the imagination is being used all the time. It implies 'see with the mind'.
Wondering Each word here is weighted with a sympathetic sense: the unknown thoughts of the animal; the natural glow of life; the creature; and the 'tiptoe' which imparts a pathetic air of loneliness.

The Faithful Swallow

A brief lyrical lament, in short lines, the poet identifying with the one bird that did not leave at the appointed time. It is a slight poem, one however that shows the usual control of the chosen form. The lines here, in their lightness and ease of sense and rhyme, almost convey the movements of the bird's wings. There is a neat variation of the couplet with alternatively rhyming lines.

As fickle they! i.e. as false as (my companions).
Fidelity i.e. loyalty.

The Robin

This poem is like that above, in that it employs a very similar technique throughout, though this one is a poem of contrasts.

There is keen observation of the habits of the robin, and an exactitude in recording sound. Notice how effective is the use of the robin as narrator. The short, quick lines emphasize the size and smoothness of the bird.

I see in pools i.e. the reflection (of the sky) in the pools.
earth as steel Again one is forced to note the effective economy of the expression.

The Puzzled Game-birds
(Triolet)

A moving short poem, which is admirably covered by the note. The form is, as we should expect, finely handled, with a plaintive and poignant reiteration of man's inhumanity to the birds he intends to use.

The Blinded Bird

Another moving poem, strongly linked in theme to the previous one. To remove one faculty is often to strengthen another, but the superbly used biblical associations of the last verse speak of the divinity of a complete thing. The repetition of the simple 'This bird' at the beginning and end of the verse is an example of a sureness of touch. The two words recall the sublimity, the miracle, of Creation.

With God's consent Note the irony.
that stab of fire i.e. the red-hot needle.
Enjailed in pitiless wire i.e. a bird-cage.
ensepulchred i.e. buried alive.

Horses Aboard

Again an identification, this time with horses being transported to a war overseas. The appraisal is cynical – they are being used – and the lines are long, in order to reflect the sombreness of the poet's mood as he contemplates horses being moved from 'the scheme Nature planned for them'. This poem might be compared with 'Drummer Hodge'.

ghast i.e. ghastly

A Sheep Fair

Two stanzas and a postscript, the form rather similar to that employed in 'Weathers' in terms of length of line, but the emphasis in the first two stanzas here is atmospheric, descriptive, while the postscript is a comment on the passage of time.

with tucked-in tails i.e. because the dogs are wet and miserably inactive.
Going–going! Note the irony: the words are a comment on all that is gone, including the auctioneer himself.
mewed band Confined.

The Roman Gravemounds

Quatrains, with alternate lines rhyming, a finely ironic comment on the past and its greatness, man's simple qualities (love of animals) in the present; yet the linking of past and present is in the expression of humanity. The irony early in the poem is a piece of self-exposure, but the poet moves on to contemplate man's ignorance of greatness and his simple expression of grief. It is a movement of the heart against the tide of history: the Hardy of domestic love, with animals as friends.

scan i.e. search.
regard i.e. estimate.

Last Words to a Dumb Friend

This is perhaps the most expressive of Hardy's animal poems, with superb control of touch; and one is tempted to say that there is a sleekness about the verse that approximates to the sleekness of the poem's subject. It exists on two levels, that of the finely descriptive on one hand, and of the contemplative, wry, ironical on the other. The fluency derives in part from an expert handling of the octosyllabic couplets.

Foot suspended in its fall Note the way that Hardy has captured the actual pose of the cat.
Never another pet Note here the anti-romantic, anti-sentimental attitude, more redolent of grief than any outward show could be.

Strange it is The whole verse is given over to the contemplation of the reversal of positions – the cat, dependent on its masters in life, yet registers as the Imperturbable in death. Hardy goes on to describe how the house itself 'Grows all eloquent of him' after he has gone.

That you moulder where you played The final comment is ironic in tone – the death of the body, the linking of life past, death present, on the same spot.

Dead 'Wessex' the Dog to the Household

The poem has a certain poignancy but even an imaginative projection into the supposed words of the dog cannot save it from some bathos – though perhaps this is deliberate. Three lines of repetition do not help to raise the level of the verse, which never reaches that of the previous poem.

as 'twere i.e. as if it were mine.

'Ah, Are You Digging on My Grave?'

A poem cleverly divided into two main parts, the words of the dead loved one and the words of the living dog. The comment is ironic, for it calls to account the whole question of the remembrance of the dead. Here both man and dog are found wanting; for the man marries another and the dog was burying a bone where his mistress has her (apparently) far from *resting* place. Terms like 'dig' and 'rest' have thus their own ironic force, and the poem is much more than its outward form, for it is almost a parody of the elegy which pays tribute to the dead. Relations and enemies alike are wholly indifferent; and the comment is that time changes everything: loyalty, love, the memory. The language is simple, for the qualities named in the previous sentence are simple ones. But the poet's appraisal of these qualities tells him that man does what he wants to do, and that the past is soon burned out in the present.

Revision questions on Descriptive and animal poems

1 Write an appreciation of any *two* of Hardy's descriptive poems, indicating the main techniques he employs.

2 By close attention to any *two* or *three* poems in this section, write an essay on Hardy's use of contrast.

3 Which do you find the most moving poem in this section and why? Write a detailed appreciation of it.

4 In what ways does Hardy make his love of animals clear? In your answer you should look closely at *three* poems.

5 In what ways could Hardy's description of nature *or* his writing of animals be described as ironic? Quote in support of your views, referring to a number of poems in your answer.

General questions

1 'He is the master of many forms.' By close reference to any *three* poems, show the variety of Hardy's verse.

Outline of points to cover in your answer

(a) *Introduction* – indicate briefly the range of Hardy's writing in this introduction to his verse – lyrical, dramatic, elegiac, ballad (short), ballad (longer narrative), song, nature poems, animal poems etc. Name perhaps the outstanding ones in each genre.

(b) Choose any *three* for detailed analysis, one in this and one each in the two following paragraphs. Example: *The Darkling Thrush* – form, images, detail, philosophy, sound, sense etc. – quote briefly and stress musicality of poem in consonance with the song of the bird. Refer particularly to the use of contrast.

(c) Example: *The Sacrilege* – form, narrative tension, dialogue, detail on rhyme scheme, refrain etc., colloquial language, essential simplicity etc.

(d) Example: *The Blinded Bird* – form, content, love of creatures, compassion, biblical reference, man's inhumanity, particular techniques (questions), etc.

(e) *Conclusion* – comparisons and contrasts in the poems, how they fit into general pattern of Hardy's verse, how they exemplify variety of subject, treatment etc.

2 Write a critical analysis of any *two* of Hardy's poems which you find particularly moving.

3 What do Hardy's poems reveal of Hardy the man? You should refer to at least *five* poems in your answer.

4 Write an essay on Hardy as the poet of local traditions.

5 How far do you consider Hardy a pessimistic poet?

6 Indicate, by reference to any *three* poems, Hardy's ability to make poetry out of slight incidents.

7 'He could always tell a good story.' Indicate whether or not this is true by referring to at least *three* poems.

8 Write an essay on two or three kinds of imagery used in Hardy's poetry.

9 Hardy was always interested in music. What evidence is there in Hardy's poetry that music played a major part in his life?

10 Write an essay either on Hardy's use of the rhyming couplet or of the quatrain in any *three* poems.

11 Write an essay on Hardy's attitude to death in any *three* poems.

12 In what ways is there a universality in Hardy's poetry? You should refer to at least *three* poems in your answer.

13 In what ways is Hardy a love poet? You should refer to a range of poetry in your answer.

14 'A craftsman with words.' How far does this comment illustrate Hardy's achievement as a poet?

15 Write on any aspect of Hardy's poetry *not* covered by the questions above but which seems to you to be important.

Further reading

The Complete Poems of Thomas Hardy ed. James Gibson, (Macmillan)

The Poems of Thomas Hardy Kenneth Marsden, (Athlone Press)

The Poetry of Thomas Hardy J. O. Bailey, (University of North Carolina Press)

Thomas Hardy Trevor Johnson, (Evans)

Thomas Hardy: A Biography Michael Millgate, (Oxford)

Young Thomas Hardy and *The Older Hardy* Robert Gittings, (Heinemann)

Pan study aids Titles published in the Brodie's Notes series

W. H. Auden Selected Poetry

Jane Austen Emma Mansfield Park Northanger Abbey Persuasion
Pride and Prejudice

Anthologies of Poetry Ten Twentieth Century Poets The Poet's Tale
The Metaphysical Poets

Samuel Beckett Waiting for Godot

Arnold Bennett The Old Wives' Tale

William Blake Songs of Innocence and Experience

Robert Bolt A Man for All Seasons

Harold Brighouse Hobson's Choice

Charlotte Brontë Jane Eyre

Emily Brontë Wuthering Heights

Robert Browning Selected Poetry

John Bunyan The Pilgrim's Progress

Geoffrey Chaucer (parallel texts editions) The Franklin's Tale
The Knight's Tale The Miller's Tale The Nun's Priest's Tale
The Pardoner's Tale Prologue to the Canterbury Tales
The Wife of Bath's Tale

Richard Church Over the Bridge

John Clare Selected Poetry and Prose

Samuel Taylor Coleridge Selected Poetry and Prose

Wilkie Collins The Woman in White

William Congreve The Way of the World

Joseph Conrad The Nigger of the Narcissus & Youth
The Secret Agent

Charles Dickens Bleak House David Copperfield Dombey and Son
Great Expectations Hard Times Little Dorrit Oliver Twist
Our Mutual Friend A Tale of Two Cities

Gerald Durrell My Family and Other Animals

George Eliot Middlemarch The Mill on the Floss Silas Marner

T. S. Eliot Murder in the Cathedral Selected Poems

J. G. Farrell The Siege of Krishnapur

Henry Fielding Joseph Andrews

F. Scott Fitzgerald The Great Gatsby

E. M. Forster Howards End A Passage to India
Where Angels Fear to Tread

William Golding Lord of the Flies The Spire

Oliver Goldsmith Two Plays of Goldsmith: She Stoops to Conquer;
The Good Natured Man

Graham Greene Brighton Rock The Power and the Glory
The Quiet American

Thom Gunn and Ted Hughes Selected Poems

Thomas Hardy Chosen Poems of Thomas Hardy
Far from the Madding Crowd Jude the Obscure
The Mayor of Casterbridge Return of the Native
Tess of the d'Urbervilles The Trumpet-Major

L. P. Hartley The Go-Between The Shrimp and the Anemone

Joseph Heller Catch-22

Ernest Hemingway For Whom the Bell Tolls
The Old Man and the Sea

Barry Hines A Kestrel for a Knave

Gerard Manley Hopkins Poetry and Prose of Gerard Manley Hopkins

Aldous Huxley Brave New World

Henry James Washington Square

Ben Jonson The Alchemist Volpone

James Joyce A Portrait of the Artist as a Young Man Dubliners

John Keats Selected Poems and Letters of John Keats

Ken Kesey One Flew over the Cuckoo's Nest

Rudyard Kipling Kim

D. H. Lawrence The Rainbow Selected Tales Sons and Lovers

Harper Lee To Kill a Mockingbird

Laurie Lee As I Walked out One Midsummer Morning
Cider with Rosie

Thomas Mann Death in Venice & Tonio Kröger

Christopher Marlowe Doctor Faustus Edward the Second

W. Somerset Maugham Of Human Bondage

Gavin Maxwell Ring of Bright Water

Thomas Middleton The Changeling

Arthur Miller The Crucible Death of a Salesman

John Milton A Choice of Milton's Verse Comus and Samson
Agonistes Paradise Lost I, II

Sean O'Casey Juno and the Paycock
The Shadow of a Gunman and the Plough and the Stars

George Orwell Animal Farm 1984

John Osborne Luther

Alexander Pope Selected Poetry

J. B. Priestley An Inspector Calls

Siegfried Sassoon Memoirs of a Fox-Hunting Man

Peter Shaffer The Royal Hunt of the Sun

William Shakespeare Antony and Cleopatra As You Like It
Coriolanus Hamlet Henry IV (Part I) Henry IV (Part II) Henry V
Julius Caesar King Lear Love's Labour's Lost Macbeth Measure for
Measure The Merchant of Venice A Midsummer Night's Dream
Much Ado about Nothing Othello Richard II Richard III Romeo and
Juliet The Sonnets The Taming of the Shrew The Tempest Twelfth
Night The Winter's Tale

G. B. Shaw Arms and the Man
Caesar and Cleopatra The Doctor's Dilemma Pygmalion Saint Joan

Richard Sheridan Plays of Sheridan: The Rivals; The Critic;
The School for Scandal

John Steinbeck The Grapes of Wrath Of Mice and Men & The Pearl

Tom Stoppard Rosencrantz and Guildenstern are Dead

J. M. Synge The Playboy of the Western World

Jonathan Swift Gulliver's Travels

Alfred Tennyson Selected Poetry

William Thackeray Vanity Fair

Flora Thompson Lark Rise to Candleford

Dylan Thomas Under Milk Wood

Anthony Trollope Barchester Towers

Mark Twain Huckleberry Finn

Keith Waterhouse Billy Liar

Evelyn Waugh Decline and Fall Scoop

H. G. Wells The History of Mr Polly The War of the Worlds

John Webster The Duchess of Malfi The White Devil

Oscar Wilde The Importance of Being Earnest

Virginia Woolf To the Lighthouse

William Wordsworth The Prelude (Books 1, 2)

William Wycherley The Country Wife

John Wyndham The Chrysalids

W. B. Yeats Selected Poetry

Pan study aids

Published jointly by Heinemann Educational Books and Pan Books

Pan Study Aids is a major new series developed to help school and college students prepare for examinations. All the authors are experienced teachers/examiners at O level, School Certificate and equivalent examinations and authors of textbooks used in schools and colleges worldwide

Each volume in the series:

- explains its subject and covers clearly and concisely and with excellent illustrations the essential points of the syllabus, drawing attention to common areas of difficulty and to areas which carry most marks in the exam

- gives guidance on how to plan revision, and prepare for the exam, outlining what examiners are looking for

- provides practice by including typical exam questions and exercises

Titles available: Physics, Chemistry, Maths, Human Biology, English Language, Geography 1 & 2, Economics, Commerce, Accounts and Book-keeping, British Government and Politics, History 1 & 2, Effective Study Skills, French, German, Spanish, Sociology